Walk on the North Side

William Primrose

Walk on the North Side

WILLIAM

PRIMROSE

Memoirs of a Violist

Brigham Young University Press

Most of the photographs in this book are from the
author's own collection. Where a photograph is used
by courtesy of another person or agency, this is
specially noted. In all cases the photographer is
noted when known.

Library of Congress Cataloging in Publication Data

Primrose, William, 1904–
    Walk on the north side.

    Discography: p.
    Includes index.
    1.   Primrose, William, 1904–   2.   Violinists,
violoncellists, etc.–Biography.   I.   Title.
ML418.P84A3   787'.1'0924 [B]   78-4952
ISBN 0-8425-1263-2 (c)
ISBN 0-8425-1313-2 (p)

Library of Congress Catalog Card Number: 78-4952
International Standard Book Number: 0-8425-1263-2 (c)
                                    0-8425-1313-2 (p)
© 1978 by Brigham Young University Press. All rights reserved
Brigham Young University Press, Provo, Utah 84602
Printed in the United States of America
4/78   1Mc, 1.5Mp   31949

Memoria in aeterna
Richard Crooks —
a noble gentleman,
a great artist,
and an unforgettable
friend

Contents

$\mathscr{Foreword}$

The robust, no-nonsense Scottish voice that speaks from the pages of this book is a refreshing contrast to the confessions of other colleagues. Where they may disguise, colour, and take some satisfaction in dramatising a situation, Bill Primrose has almost the opposite approach. He reduces it to the bare bones, but in so doing we are entertained and enriched by the frankness of statement and the witty gift of bringing punctured balloons down to earth. Thus motives are not glorified, personages are not idolised, and music and musicians take their place as useful but not overromanticised elements in good, simple, straightforward living which includes boxing, soccer, golf, chess, chemistry, and a well-rounded catholic appreciation of all that goes into life—so often musicians are considered to be hothouse plants; decidedly this is not the case with Bill—and even gambling, in which our careers are identical (for we both played once and won, though I only a modest five Swiss francs, and the second time we lost and never played again).

Nor was Bill's musical career an exclusive one of concert performances, for he also played at banquets and civic affairs, in fact, wherever they could use a viola, paralleling the extraordinary experience of Piatigorsky in Berlin nightclubs and Sasha Schneider in Polish brothels. Certainly he did not have a sheltered upbringing!

Yet it was not cunning nor the survival instinct that made Bill Primrose finally decide to be a violist rather than a violinist. It was rather that intuitive English penchant for the centre of harmony which the viola represents in our music, the English really having created musical harmony—witness Dowland and Purcell—and social harmony too. It is the English avoidance of prima donna exposure in terms of virtuoso exhibitionism, the English preference for the inner voice, and, therefore, Tertis, Primrose, and the present great flowering of the viola as an instrument on its own. If Tertis was the first protagonist, Bill Primrose was certainly the first star of the viola, and when he speaks of the reluctance of conductors to engage him because of not wishing to offend their own first violist, it is understandable, because when he began his viola career violists were not yet stars and the margin between the first violist of the orchestra and the solo violist was fairly close in status, if not ability—certainly not as great as that between the concertmaster and the solo violinist, neither in terms of public drawing-power nor the repertoire. Now this is rapidly changing and there are several star challengers today on the viola.

I share several things with Bill beyond our gambling: his feeling about the magic of a London wartime summer, his admiration for Oscar Shumsky as one of the great violinists and teachers, and his evaluation of competitions. Although I do chair the City of London Carl Flesch Competition, Yfrah Neaman's and my aim is to make it as little competitive as possible and as rewarding as possible to all those who participate by giving them the opportunity of discussing their playing and their future with the members of the jury. It is not only a competition but an assessment of different musical, human, and technical qualities which may not always be realised in the same person.

I am happy to report that through a miraculous treatment by Dr. Noguchi of Japan Bill's hearing has been restored. This is not only a great joy for him but for the whole musical world. May he be with us many years, sharing his music, his wit, and his great gifts as a teacher.

Yehudi Menuhin

Preface

Whenever I spy a book by a colleague gracing a bookseller's shelves, I immediately turn to the index. If my name is not among those present, I restrain any urge to buy the book. How my old friend Gregor Piatigorsky contrived to exclude me from the text of his otherwise amusing reminiscences, I'll never know. It must have caused him considerable effort. I don't wish to appear conceited, but our paths did so frequently cross. Of course I read his book. It came as a gift from a friend. And a Scotsman will read any and all books he finds in his Christmas stocking.

There are those, however, who could complain about my not having mentioned them in the following pages. My urge to include many names in addition to those that already grace the pages of my memoirs stems, I fear, from a motive of doubtful nobility and repute. But I do regret that I have not mentioned a number of persons and personalities or written more about those who are but cursorily mentioned. Yehudi Menuhin springs to mind at once.

Though he may not know it, I was the first to see the letter that his mentor, the late Louis Persinger, wrote to Ysaÿe concerning the child and the wonder of him in 1926 when I was a student. I have so much more to tell too about Feuermann and the charming and great artist Pierre Fournier. I would like to have spent more time with my most amiable and kind boss at Curtis Institute, Efrem Zimbalist, and his wife, the former Mary Curtis Bok, truly one of the last of the "great ladies." In this connection—the Curtis Institute—I would have wished to add much more about that distinguished alumnus Henri Temianka, whose friendship I value. The incandescent, incontrovertible, incorruptible, indisputable Scot; and don't we have it from that faithworthy source, Thomas Beecham, that the name is really Tam O'Shanter!

Since completing the first rough draft of this book I have spent most of my time in Japan. And about that sweet magic an entire volume might easily be written; a short, or even long, chapter would hardly do it justice. But time runs on.

That there are as many pages as there are in this present volume is largely to the credit of David Dalton, my friend, former student, and colleague. I cannot thank him enough for his tireless encouragement, support, and numerous contributions to the writing of this book. I am also greatly indebted to Brigham Young University, Provo, Utah, for the pleasant circumstances under which most of these pages were initially written. And I thank Kerril Sue Rollins for refining my writing and rendering it more readable, Thomas J. Mathiesen for checking the accuracy of references to compositions and other technical elements of the manuscript, and Arnold Logie, editor at Brigham Young University Press, for his personal interest and careful attention as the finished manuscript became a published book.

Quite often as I have been recounting, upon request, some of the incidents contained in the following pages, someone has commented, "You must put this in writing." I finally decided to do just that—to write down for the public many of the interesting and true stories of my career as a violist and also some of my personal philosophy of performing and teaching. This book is the result.

All books of this type usually call for a list of the artist's recordings, whether or not they are still available to the record-buying public. I have included in the appendix a list of mine, most of which are not now obtainable. I have a splendid solution to this problem, however. The reader can catch a flight to Haneda airport in Tokyo and, if he wisely does not overburden himself with baggage, take the train to Hamamatsuchō, change there to the Yamanote Line for Yurakuchō, walk a couple of blocks to the Tokyo Municipal Subway, board at Hibiya station, disembark at Jinbōchō, and, ascending to street level, find himself on a boulevard lined with the most astounding conglomeration of second-hand bookstores it has ever been my privilege to browse through. He will find books in almost every language and condition. Now and then he may also come across a shop that sells recordings long deleted from the catalog. There he can find the Primrose recordings. But at a price. Some few months ago I saw displayed as the centerpiece of the window front of one of these *caves de trésors* an old Pathé recording of the *Havanaise* of Saint-Saëns as recorded by Jacques Thibaud. The price? One hundred U.S. dollars. And so it goes for Primrose.

Primrose in America in the early 1940s

1

The North
Side of 57th
Street

At the end of my fourth season with the NBC Symphony in 1941 the word went around that Toscanini was resigning and would not continue his association with the corporation. I believed that some passage of arms had occurred between the maestro and the powers at the National Broadcasting Company and I was quite convinced that, being a man of such great strength of character and implacable disposition, he would not return. Having joined the orchestra to gain the experience of really high-grade orchestral playing under the directorship of the prestigious Toscanini, I now felt that I had accomplished what I had set out to do. Furthermore, I didn't particularly wish to play under any other conductor. It's not that I thought another conductor would not be fine enough or interesting enough to work with; during my tenure I had played under Bruno Walter, Stokowski, Steinberg, and others. I simply felt I had served my apprenticeship.

Having made up my mind to return to the solo world, I made quite certain that people knew I was going to be available. In other words when someone inquired, "What are you doing these days?" I would respond with, "I'm resigning from the NBC Symphony." The reaction was usually, "You're doing the best thing you could possibly do for yourself. You are definitely taking a step in the right direction." This left me wondering: That's all very well and good, but don't you have anything up your sleeve to offer me? At the time there was really not very much in sight.

I have often been asked by ambitious parents, who bring their youngsters to audition for me, to advise them on how to begin building a career. I astound not a few when I admonish them to walk on the north side of 57th Street. There is very good reason for my counsel.

At the time I was a member of the NBC Symphony I was also a member of the Lotos Club in New York, the premises of which were then on the south side of 57th Street, next to the Great Northern Hotel. Invariably, after we finished our morning rehearsal, I walked over to the club for lunch, proceeding up 6th Avenue and turning west on 57th on the south side of the street. One day, however, as I turned west I looked across to the Steinway Building and saw in the window a rather unusual portrait of Rachmaninoff. I went over to have a better look at it and, having done so, was turning on my heel to return to the club when I ran into that incomparable tenor, Richard Crooks, and his wife, Mildred.

I knew Crooks because the London String Quartet (LSQ), of which I had been a member, had collaborated with him in some joint recitals. Also, it had been my duty, and sundry of my colleagues', to play in the orchestra that performed for the "Voice of Firestone" broadcast when Crooks was the regular weekly singer, and I got to know him better through that association.

He asked me the question that so many were asking, "What are you doing these days?" I told him and he commended my action, patting me on the back. Then, to my very pleasant surprise, instead of just turning and walking away with no further consideration of my future as the others had done, he said, "Do you think by any chance you might be in California at the beginning of next year?"

I really hadn't the slightest idea where I was going to be, but I didn't say that. I knew something was in the wind and I answered, "Yes, quite possibly. Why do you ask?"

He replied that he was becoming rather tired of making lengthy, arduous tours and carrying a whole program by himself and he would like to have someone assist him. It had just occurred to him that if I were in California he could use me in the west coast con-

A debonair-looking Primrose

Primrose and David Dalton working on the manuscript for this book

certs. By that time I had definitely made up my mind that I was going to be in California. He told me to get in touch with his manager.

After several very friendly conversations with manager Horace Parmelee and the Columbia Artists management I found out that Crooks wanted me for the entire tour, which, instead of being a mere baker's dozen in California, turned out to be over forty concerts from east to west. Here I was, touring with the most popular singer of the day and playing to audiences of 2,500 to 3,000 people a night, most of whom had never even heard of a viola, other than the one which, like the primrose, might flourish in a garden!

Much later, when Crooks had retired to California and I had given myself over to concert work on my own, I reminded him of the day we met on 57th Street and asked him, "If we hadn't met, would you have sought me out?"

"No," he said, "it just came to my mind when I spoke to you."

When I admonish anyone aspiring to a career to walk on the north side of 57th Street, I simply imply tht he should never become so frustrated or so despondent that when opportunity arrives he is not ready for it. In my circumstances at the time I could easily have felt that nothing was going to come my way, that there was no use practicing—no use doing anything. But it just so happened that I was ready and I was on the right side—the north side—of the street.

Primrose at age 12, on the occasion of his first concert, with the Mendelssohn concerto, in St. Andrew's Hall, Glasgow

2

Early Years in Glasgow

My earliest childhood recollections are of watching my father teaching violin at home in the "parlor" of our exceedingly small apartment at No. 18 Wilton Drive in Glasgow. When I returned there—where I was born on August 23, 1904—I, like many who have traveled far and wide and then return home, found that what once appeared to be a commodious parlor now actually seemed impossible, even lilliputian—the combination of a piano (though an upright), a dining table, a couch, easy chairs, and other furnishings in that room where I picked up all my early knowledge of the rudiments of violin playing.

As an infant I often sat on the floor with a wooden stick in each hand—one, of course, represented the violin and the other the bow—and copied my father's movements as he played. When he, relishing my apparent enthusiasm, bought and placed a quartersized violin in my eager hands in 1908, I began at once really to play. My only mistake in the execution of a scale of two octaves was that I

7

Primrose at age 3

played—following the open G string—the succeeding notes A, B, C, and D with my four fingers and repeated the D (fourth finger closed note) with the open D before essaying a similar ascent a fifth higher. Such are the intimations of precocity!

My childhood was probably quite similar to that of any other boy on the street where I lived. But I resented the differences imposed on me by musical chores. Because my early studies in that field came quite easily to me, why be obliged to practice something I felt I could already do well enough when I might be out of doors practicing something like soccer, in which I felt inferior to some of my school playmates? Some years later I became aware that I did not know as much about my musical trade as puerile conceit had led me to suppose. My dedication to practice did not burgeon fully

Camillo Ritter, Primrose's early teacher

until I came under the ponderous, yet benign, influence of my great master, Eugene Ysaÿe, of whom I will say more later.

I did practice enough, however, to make public appearances with reasonable acclaim from about the age of twelve. But the diligent, painstaking, sedulous era came years later when, turning from aimless ways, I associated myself with the many ambitious youngsters who assembled each summer at the appropriately named villa "La Chanterelle" (the E string of the violin) of Ysaÿe at Le Zoute on the Belgian coast.

My father's anxiety in my behalf was that I should enjoy the musical benefits that had escaped his early experience. He hoped that what appeared to him to presage a distinguished career might bring opportunities that would enable me to achieve the goals he had failed to achieve. He was entranced (and that is the only word I can find to describe his lifetime love affair with the violin) with all that appertained to string playing and pedagogy. He had a profound knowledge of the history of string instruments and their makers. It was grievous to him that until the termination of his adolescence he had wasted his time, in his opinion, in the tea trade as a tea taster. In my judgment, however, this was but a foretoken of his good taste in every musical connection.

My father was wise enough to perceive that it would not be appropriate for him to instruct his child in the difficult art of violin playing. And so he arranged for me to become a pupil of Camillo Ritter, an Austrian national who had studied with Joachim and Ševčik and who was the most prominent teacher of violin in Scotland at the time. David McCallum, father of the television actor, was a contemporary of mine in Ritter's class and we were rivals at the time. David, Sr., became prominent in the orchestra field and was Beecham's concertmaster for years in the Royal Philharmonic. He was there when I recorded Berlioz's *Harold in Italy* with Sir Thomas in 1953.

When I joined Ritter's class in 1908, I entered into my first regular, organized study. Ritter put me through a rigorous and arduous course of work—all Ševčik for months on end and all meticulously planned. For respite I was assuaged with Raff's notorious Cavatina and took an immediate dislike to this piece of musical sorghum. A concerto in G major by de Bériot I found gracious and charming. Otherwise Ševčik prevailed. In the manner of so many other compilers of textbooks dealing with technical development, Ševčik offered little in the way of textual explanation. The Ševčik method came in the form of a sort of "oral tradition" handed down from generation to generation; and through Ritter's connection with Ševčik I was, in a manner, of the first generation.

I was given the usual diet of études and scales with an ever increasing dose of the standard literature. And I was beginning to develop my own taste in music. I could work up no enthusiasm for the cantabile theme of the Paganini Concerto in D. The Ernst F-sharp minor concerto likewise irked me. My dislike did not grow out of the formidable technical problems. My revulsion to the thematic material was not a sort of self-induced "escape clause." Another work that seemed tawdry was *Zigeunerweisen*. But of course I had to perform it on occasion. I enjoyed many other Sarasate pieces much more—especially, years later, a suite for violin entitled *Sarasateana*, which Efrem Zimbalist had put together for violin and

10

piano and later transcribed for me to perform on the viola. The piano part of this suite is an exemplary model of how to improve, in an enchanting and sophisticated manner, the rather jejune accompaniments offered by Sarasate.

Of the works I enjoyed, Joseph Joachim's Variations for Violin and Orchestra had a profound effect on me and never ceased to engage my affections. There was nothing chauvinistic about my liking for Dr. Joachim's rather aristocratic work nor for his Hungarian Concerto, though my teacher was one of his students. My inclination toward all music that came my way, either as a performer or as a listener, was inspired by an instinctive selectivity. Whether my instincts were approved did not matter to me at all. If mine were not agreeable to others, that only meant to me that we add to the broad *tertium quid* that divides us all.

It had been arranged by Professor Ritter for me to go to Prague in 1914 to study with Ševčik. I was to stay with the professor's sister and her family.* I was only nine or ten at the time and terribly excited at the thought of traveling to a foreign country with exotic mores and customs. But then, to my great disappointment and to the disappointment of my father and Professor Ritter, word came from his sister that I must not travel to Prague. An epidemic of some sort had broken out. Professor Ritter's sister was a prominent woman and acquainted with many people of note, and I have often thought since that she knew there was a war threatening and this was her way of sparing me from it. I was told to "keep off the grass" and thus my excursion to foreign delights and experiences was aborted.

Both my father and teacher had the practice in common of never recognizing my talent or precociousness, at least in my presence. On the contrary, Ritter, my father, and other dour Scots admonished me continually to remember at all times that I was not to get above myself and that I was to understand that I was not as good as I might believe I was. An impossible way to nurture the burgeoning prodigy!

I experienced but a few sonata sessions, as the worthy pianists resident in Glasgow weren't especially interested in playing with a youngster of little repute. I sometimes performed in concerts at our Congregational church, where my father attended services regularly and where his sister sang in the choir. Once, to the astonishment of everybody, I won a prize for Bible knowledge at Sunday School.

---

*Mme Ritter Bondi, a distinguished pianist of her era.

Primrose at age 8, Christmas 1912

The prize was Dickens's *Child's History of England,* which I have cherished beyond all subsequent histories which informed my passionate interest. No one had suspected I had any religious bent at all, but on that day some choice spirit invested me with unusual ability and I answered all the questions correctly.

Occasionally I was persuaded to play at schools in Glasgow; but when, with sullen feet, I entered the schoolroom to perform, I knew that I had touched bottom. The setting wasn't right. I often played at the Palette Club in Glasgow, the membership of which was made up of people who were interested in the arts. It was something similar to the "Savage Club" in London or the "Players" in New York, both of which I am a member. They had rather nice premises—a large room with a platform on which rested a fine piano and an off-stage room where one could warm up. In short, the atmosphere was congenial, perhaps too nice for some of the pieces I was obliged to play. I even sank so low as to play Raff's Cavatina, which I abhorred.

I was never able to feel comfortable performing unless the setting was as correct and appropriate as I found it at the Palette Club, for example. I have been like this all my life, and it sometimes proves to be a drawback. I know many musicians who can approach their instrument with enviable aplomb in any situation and in any surrounding, and play. I can't. I remember years later listening to Oscar Shumsky perform one night in a *ship's lounge.* The NBC Symphony, of which he and I were members, was on its way to South America and Toscanini was in the audience. I was envious and admired him so to be able to play under such conditions. I don't know if this is an overblown sense of order, fitness, or something else on my part. I just have to be aware of the proper *ambiente* for a concert performance.

My introduction to chamber music didn't come until later I went to London. Few people in Glasgow would sit down and play string quartets for pleasure alone. This rather astonished me, because the town was so very musical and had such a number of excellent players. Ritter, however, had a quartet that for a while met on Sunday mornings and my father played as violist in the group.

The musical culture of Glasgow seemed to be preeminently represented by the Scottish Orchestra, of which my father was a member. I heard it conducted first by Emil Mlynarsky, the father of the present Mrs. Artur Rubinstein. Following him came Landon Ronald, a very popular conductor, a composer of some derivative merit, and a fine pianist, who accompanied Nellie Melba for years. Ronald was also the head, or principal, of the Guildhall School of Music, and it was he who eventually brought me to that school in London to study. After Landon Ronald some quite distinguished musicians came to conduct the orchestra—Sir John Barbirolli and George Szell, among others. The orchestra was well supported and there was interesting music-making, particularly because of the number of German musicians who had come to Scotland to make their home and afford (I might even suggest *condescend*) their services to the orchestra.

At that time if a man was a German and carried a fiddle case he was a minor genius in our eyes. A German could do no wrong musically, as far as the Glasgow public was concerned, much to the annoyance of Scottish musicians. At the outbreak of World War I, however, the Germans simply evanesced! My recollections of this are fairly vivid. My teacher, an Austrian, was naturalized, and his wife was the daughter of a very distinguished Glasgow physician. Nevertheless, he was Austrian born and his sympathies were with the Central Powers. He, of course, kept his opinions very much to himself.

For me, a small boy, this was all very thrilling, and I would have given anything to have gone to battle myself, to have embarked on a marvelous adventure. One of the newspaper placards displayed a *very large* Russian soldier—his size was meant to depict the number of Russians at the disposal of the Allies—a *large* German soldier, next to him, a *not-quite-so-large* French soldier, and, clear down the line, a *very small* British soldier. We were supposed to gain solace from this by adding together the heights of all the allied men and seeing by how much the German was over-topped. That was very reassuring for us—but naively so.

The gloom brought on by World War I seemed somewhat mitigated by happy musical events. I still recall many of the artists and the happenings surrounding their appearances. My father went every summer with the family to Blackpool, a coastal resort in Lancashire, to play the season, which consisted of vaudeville-type theater on week nights and symphony concerts on Sundays with Landon Ronald conducting. I remember the excitement of the preparations for these journeys. To my child's sense of proportion these preparations seemed massive. There was the packing of the hampers and the bags and the calling for the cab on the day of departure—the cab with the spavined old horse and an equally spavined old driver, always with a scruffy top hat on his head and a rug around his knees. Together we all traveled in the cab with its peculiar smell of horse's stale and decayed straw.

Later, just before I went to London, my father played a couple of seasons on the Isle of Man in the Irish Sea. Our voyage was most insecure. German U-boats were prowling around at the time, and with the exception of my father the whole family got revoltingly seasick. Poor father had to take each of us in turn to the rail of the ship, let us unload, help us back, and then pick up the next patient. This wild journey lasted for about five hours.

The working class in Lancashire were very musical. During their vacation, which curiously enough was called a "wake" in native dialect, they came to Blackpool and the Isle of Man to sport on the beaches, consume inordinate amounts of hot potato pie—"sup ale" as the vernacular had it—guffaw at the faint bawdiness of vaudeville, and hear the visiting opera singers and other stars on Sundays. Lancashire is rival to Yorkshire, just as Glasgow is always the rival to Edinburgh. The rivalry embraced all measure of contention: soccer; intervarsity rugby football, played without heed to life or limb; and, of course, music, which was held in as much regard as it was, and is, by the Welsh. There I heard singers such as Caruso and Emmy Destinn and the great violinists of the day—Ysaÿe, Kubelik, Elman, Kreisler, and Szigeti. This was in 1909, and I can still hear their respective sounds in my inmost ear, with the exception of Kubelik's. I have no recollection of Kubelik's sound whatever, just his dark and saturnine appearance—and his long black hair.

Kriesler stood like a young hussar, with his black mustache and his pose strict with discipline. When I first heard him, he played the Mendelssohn concerto. Before he got his violin up during the one-and-one-half-bar introduction, my mother declared, "I'm going to enjoy this!" That was the essence of the man—before Kreisler started to play, one knew one was going to delight in it. "Sweets with sweet war not, joy delights in joy." Szigeti played the Bruch G minor, as I recall, and I went backstage afterward to meet him. I had the audacity to ask him his age, and he told me he was seventeen.

All of these people appeared in Glasgow too. And I heard the London String Quartet there, years before I became a member. They played the Brahms Quartet Op. 67 the first time I ever heard it, and I almost went out of my mind as I encountered such sweet joy. A revelation. Glasgow also had a very famous choir, appropriately named the Orpheus Choir, that engaged many soloists to assist in its programs. The choir was conducted by Hugh Roberton, a

Primrose's father, John Primrose

mortician. He eventually became Sir Hugh, not because of his successful undertaking, I hasten to say, but because of his contribution of great merit to music.

And now for a little more on my family. I have sometimes been asked if I descended from one of the clans. The Primroses are a Lowland family; no Highland blood enlivens our veins. The sachem of the family, so to speak, is Lord Rosebery, whose family name is Primrose. A very distinguished personage was the late *Fifth* Earl. In England it is customary to place a blue plaque on the outside wall of any house where a notable person has lived. When I wandered in the august realms of Mayfair in the West End of London, I often

Primrose's mother, Margaret-McInnis Whiteside Primrose

saw the inscription "Here lived Archibald Philip Primrose, 5th Earl of Rosebery." My father told me that Rosebery had three ambitions in life: (1) to be Prime Minister, (2) to win the Derby, and (3) to marry the wealthiest woman in Europe. He fulfilled all three. Whether the particular Rothschild whom he married was the wealthiest woman in Europe, I don't know, but I doubt if she had to be much concerned about her dress allowance.

During my childhood there was not a terribly strong relationship between parents and their offspring. In Scotland at that period, I think in England also, the bond between parent and child was never noticeably intimate. The slogan in those days was "Children should be seen but not heard," which I think could well apply today. But it was overdone in my time, and the parent-child relationship was akin to aloofness. The parents were always King and Queen of the House and their children the humble subjects. It was not that a schism existed between parents and children. There were just not the close family ties of affection that I observed when I first came to the United States.

The aloofness of which I speak was simply a result of tradition—that tradition John Kenneth Galbraith, originally from a Scottish family, though born in Canada, has spoken about, with particular regard to family life in Scotland. I believe my grandfathers on both sides were even more dominant in their families than my father was in his. My father arrived at the time when women started to rebel against the tyranny of the father as the head of the family. My mother was among those women, and father probably suffered because of the old, withering tradition of the domineering father as the hub around which the family revolved.

I am the eldest of three children. My young brother resides in England and my sister Jean in New York. Jean is a very talented painter and illustrator and has made these skills her life's work. During World War II my brother and sister remained in London with my parents.

My mother's family was more musically engaged than my father's. Her brother, Samuel Whiteside, achieved a distinguished position for himself in the musical life of Glasgow. He played several instruments, including violin, and was prominent in the profession. I don't recall him; he drowned accidentally when I was quite a small boy. But he was the strong musical link between the two families, the Whitesides and the Primroses.

My mother came to America frequently and was visiting me in the United States just a few months before her death in 1962 at the

18

age of eighty-nine. On her first transatlantic voyage I thought she might be a passenger in the Athenia, the first passenger ship sunk by the Germans immediately after the clash of arms in 1939. I was excused from my NBC Symphony duties at the time to haunt the docks in New York day upon day, waiting for a British ship to arrive to see if I could find her. It was impossible to obtain any information on passenger lists and ship schedules. That would have constituted a breach of war security. I simply had to go to the docks and wait.

My father's passing from this life affected me deeply. I hadn't seen him since the second holocaust afflicted Great Britain in 1939—and most of the rest of the world subsequently. I was filled with admiration that amounted to awe as I listened nightly to Ed Murrow inimitably describe the sufferings, the fortitude, the almost fatalistic sense of humor that glorified the inhabitants of London during that period known as the "Battle of Britain." By this time, many years earlier in fact, my father, mother, sister, and brother had settled themselves in the camp of my father's enemy. He pitched his tent of his own volition in London among the "hosts of Anglia" and endeavored to live out his prideful life without emerging more than he had to in order to earn his way. This he did with no notable success, financially speaking.

Concerning our relationship I fancy there were two great disappointments in his life. He, like many of his friends, was an ardently nationalistic Scot and was often cast into Caledonian gloom because I didn't follow in his chauvinistic footsteps. His thoughts were bitterly slanted where the Sassenach intruded. Along with this the fact that my first wife was an Englishwoman cast a spell of anguish and estrangement between us that lasted for some years. So might a Talmudic Jew have felt if his son had married a shiksa. I have always looked with a disapproving eye on nationalism of any sort.

The second cause of estrangement was my ultimate attachment to the viola. Although my father "doubled" on this instrument, he always felt that anyone who was confined to play out his musical life on what he regarded the secondary instrument did but confess his failure as a violinist. And to be sure, in his day this was often the case. Who among string players does not recall that in Germany at that time the Bratsche was more often than not referred to as the Penzioninstrument? When considered too old, too decrepit, or too immoral to play the violin (and heaven knows that takes a bit of doing), the violinist was relegated to scrape out the winter of his

Primrose's parents at the Southend Pier, 1939

discontent as a violist. Needless to say, I did not share my father's feelings about the viola. I regarded all string instruments as a sort of archipelago; none of them was an island unto itself.

During the war years my father and I became closer through our exchange of letters, despite the continued presence of the *shiksa* in the "family portrait," as it were. After the defeat of Hitler I took off on a tour of South America and the Caribbean Islands. Letters at that time, of course, were often slow in reaching their destinations. The last letter from my father found me in Bogotá long after its dispatch from London. Together with my reply from Ciudad Trujillo in Santo Domingo a short time later, this was the final communication we had.

I was living at that time in Philadelphia, where I was a faculty member of the Curtis Institute of Music. Reaching my point of repose in that City of Brotherly Love after a fatiguing tour, I started to contact my many friends by telephone. One of these happened to be an old friend of the family, who had settled there many years earlier. When I introduced myself by telephone, he informed me that he had recently received word of my father's death. In the circumstances that prevailed at the moment, it was a shock to me. The letter from my mother with the dolorous news was at the time chasing me around the various Latin American republics I had recently visited.

About Glasgow, the city of my youth, I remember it as a dingy city, an industrial town. But we all had a great pride in ourselves and used to revile the Edinburgh snobs, as we called them, with "The Lord gaed us a guid conceit o' ourselves." Edinburgh, the Royal City of Scotland, is a beautiful town. Glasgow was a rough place, with striving racial mixtures, very vital and alive. The Jewish and Polish populations were large. Many Poles had been recruited to work in the coal mines. The Irish population was sizable also, and a number of feuds and battles royal took place. Added to those ethnic mixtures was a large "whisky" population that really set things afire, especially on Hogmanay (New Year's Eve). Glasgow was also full of smog, a result of the soft coal that was burned and the lowering climate. All I distinctly recall of the winters there is breathing this foul air.

After many years I returned to Glasgow in December 1968. The Scottish BBC, at the instance of its then musical director, Dr. Watson Forbes, a distinguished violist in his own right, organized a viola competition in honor of me. It was limited to young British and Commonwealth players resident in Great Britain. Along with some

21

Primrose the international artist

22

of my English viola-playing colleagues I had to adjudicate the finalists. I noticed at the time that the Glasgow Corporation must really have gotten to work on the smog pestilence, for there was no smog at all. Glasgow had become a most attractive city. Knowing that American cities have the same problem and being interested in how Glasgow had solved theirs, I asked the mayor, the Lord Provost as he is called, "How did you do it?" to which he answered in his very Scottish brogue, "We made antipollution laws and we made them obey the laws!"

The educational standards in Scotland were notably high, and so aside from music I had of necessity my academic interests. It seemed that a very large part of the year was taken up with school; probably it wasn't, but it appeared that way. It seemed endless. Besides this I must confess that my interests were mostly in sports. I played a lot of soccer and stupidly later decided to box. Although this was not bare-knuckle fighting, just the regular amateur stuff with gloves, I was fortunate never to have injured my hands. I could very easily have done irreparable injury. I didn't engage in any of the whisky brawls. That sort of thing terrified me. It is a strange thing, but whenever I watched a couple of fellows box in the ring I felt I could go in myself and box. When I saw two men fight with bare fists and in hot blood in the street, however, I became nauseated and almost threw up. It horrified me.

I became in my youth a voracious reader and have remained so. I loved Dickens and Thackeray but couldn't abide Scott because he was invariably a school project. I always found that with Sir Walter I had to read some fifty pages before I reached the narrative proper. I enjoyed most subjects and learned quickly; but since I did not have to work too hard, nothing really became well founded. It is the same with me in regard to foreign languages. To paraphrase somebody, I can make myself misunderstood in about six of these. I had an ear for languages, however; and if I had had to work hard, I would have become a good linguist.

The only thing I really worked at besides music was chess. This I did because a certain individual constantly prevailed and sneered at me and crowed over me as he did so. It heated my young blood, which was hot enough already, and I thought: I'm going to work hard and get him! And I did. I resented very few subjects. I found chemistry fascinating. When we did elementary chemistry, I thought I could somehow or other blow up the whole school. And I was entranced by the consequence of such an eruption: no more school—perpetual vacation with unceasing soccer.

The old Guildhall School of Music, John Carpenter Street, London

3

*Student
Days in
London*

In 1919 I was prodded into playing for Landon Ronald, later Sir
Landon, who was then conducting the Scottish Orchestra. He was
sufficiently impressed by my playing to arrange with the Corporation of the City of London to grant me a scholarship to the Guildhall School of Music, of which he was principal. And thus I descended from the grim fastnesses of Caledonia, stern and wild, to
reside among the Sassenachs. On my arrival I displayed my adoles-
cent wares for some of the school's bigwigs whom Ronald had
summoned for the occasion.

I wasn't fully prepared and my wares were somewhat tarnished. I
could see that Ronald was disappointed. He was loyal to his con-
victions, however, and explained to those assembled that my father
had just undergone serious surgery; obviously his son was concerned. That was not true. I was not at an age to be concerned
about things like that, especially as I had an unshakable faith in
Scottish surgeons and was perfectly certain my father would survive

25

*Sir Landon Ronald, British conductor, who saved the day of
Primrose's audition in London*

his operation, which he did. I was so excited to be in London that I
simply neglected to practice. Before leaving Glasgow I had studied
the map of London for months, so thoroughly in fact that I, the
"outlander," was able to give directions to people who inquired of
me from time to time. I explored everywhere and almost walked
myself off my none-too-well-shod feet.

Because my father had been well established in Glasgow, I often
wondered if my family had made the wisest move in following me
to London. I suppose they came to preserve the winsome purity of
my puberty, among other things. My father was a member of the
working class, earning little money, as was the case with most orchestra musicians then. It was some time before he was able to

break into the orchestra field in London. As in any other place in the world, there was a clique, and to have leaped that barrier would have taken a great deal more *chutzpah* than my modest, honest father ever possessed. My family lived in a rather critical situation for a while; after the war it was difficult to find living accommodations in London. Father was never a good businessman and was easily overawed by people who put on a show of any kind. We finally found an apartment owned by an ex-soldier, a colonel—a "temporary gentleman," as I believe other than members of the regular army officers corps were alluded to then—who I suspect was desperate to divest himself of an unbearable debt and who knew how to appraise a nice guy. My poor father was overwhelmed by his calculated condescension and agreed to everything that was asked of him in the sale. It took him a long time to recover from that experience.

In contrast to the rather considerable academic burden imposed on a student by present-day college curricula, my life was rather free and easy at the Guildhall School of Music. It was very similar to the life of a young man of wealth and class who went to Oxford or Cambridge, except that I didn't have the wealth, and the "class" was latent. He wasn't *obliged* to attend lectures. He could do exactly as he wished until his exam ominously loomed. Then he would seek the aid of a "crammer" and try to bone up on a term's work in a few days. I was supposed to take secondary piano, theory, and counterpoint, but I skipped them all. The reason here, as in the case of my poor application to languages, was my ear. If I had been given something in the way of advanced harmony and counterpoint, I might have been interested. But everything started from the *fons et origo*; and when I was told that the leading tone had to go to the tonic or that I musn't double thirds or "commit" consecutive fifths I thought it a waste of time, since my ear had informed me of this already. I had had sufficient aural experience with music to be aware of this beforehand. This was a very callow attitude I must now admit, but at that period I wasn't interested in glimpses of the obvious.

I was also cocky when it came to the piano. I was so far ahead with the violin that I refused to demean my ego and start playing simple studies on the piano. I had a very pleasant and gentle teacher, but he was much too forgiving. I got about as far as *Für Elise* by Beethoven and that was it. I have regretted this ever since. I would give anything to be able to play now. Whenever I heard Kreisler or Heifetz play the piano, I was profoundly envious. In a present-day

27

school of music one is definitely constrained to give attention to piano, theory, and counterpoint; otherwise there will be serious repercussions. In my day we just weren't obliged to. As I have mentioned, I knew by ear what was correct and what was incorrect. I had already done some work along these lines in Glasgow and quite a bit of performing, which always helps.

My violin instructor in London was Max Mossel, a Dutchman, and frankly not a good teacher. He knew everybody who was worth knowing, and most people in the world of strings knew him in turn. He managed a series of concerts in Great Britain called the Max Mossel Concerts and spent more time in his entrepreneurial chores than in listening to his student of the moment. I must admit that I was so little inspired by violin instruction at the Guildhall School that I kept in the cloakroom a volume of concertos edited by Joachim, which I would retrieve before my lesson and read in class. And that would be my lesson for the day. I was then and always have been an adept and instant reader. In 1923 I made my debut in Queens Hall, and I remember Professor Mossel urging me the day before to "hope for the best." I thought it a desultory way to send a youngster off on his musical hegira.

The violin I played on at the debut was the Betts Strad now reposing in the Library of Congress. It belonged to a friend of my father who lived in Glasgow. He was a sort of "Heinz" of Scotland and produced all sorts of soups, sauces, and sausages. He also developed a penchant for collecting fine string instruments and eventually sold his entire collection to an American collector in the mid-1920s. I laid claim as well to a violin belonging to my father—a Nicolas Gagliano, 1735—that he purchased before the turn of the century from a firm in Glasgow for ninety pounds. The prices of string instruments had soared in the meantime. After my father's death some thirty years ago I sold the Gagliano to Norman Carroll, the present concertmaster of the Philadelphia Orchestra. I believe my father bought his Amati viola for about eighty pounds, and I later sold it in 1951 to Ferenc Molnar, the former solo violist for the San Francisco Symphony, for many times that sum. The Andreas Guarneri, which I now own, was sold to Lord Harrington in the 1890s for a relatively trivial sum.

Landon Ronald was of the greatest assistance in making my debut possible. I had been earning a scanty living playing at banquets given by the city companies. These guilds, or livery companies, had been formed hundreds of years ago; among them were the Vintners Company and the Ropemakers Company. The Vintners Company

28

was not made up entirely of men in the wine trade, nor were the Ropemakers men who did nothing but make rope. They were people who were influential in the business world and in many cases people with some leaning toward the arts. The guild residences, or "halls," were in connection with the Guildhall School of Music and were quite remarkable. They were comprised of very old buildings with beautiful premises, usually one or two marvelous Adam ceilings, and other architectural magnificences. It is so long since I have lived in London memory may have played me false in reciting some of the above facts. But I believe the reader has the picture!

The occasions were very formal. As a rule some form of musical entertainment took place at the conclusion of dinner. I played, for example, for the Worshipful Company of Musicians, made up almost entirely of nonmusicians. I was, in fact, awarded their silver medal, an honor of no little distinction, the previous award having gone to the late Sir Eugene Goossens. At this particular dinner Landon Ronald made a speech, pleading for funds that would enable me to play a couple of concerts in London. Giving a concert with orchestra in Queens Hall cost the sort of money that was quite beyond my father's means. The funds were placed in trust and I duly played my debut concert with Ronald conducting. A week later a recital at Wigmore Hall set me on my way. About two years later, to my gratification and surprise, the balance of the fund was transferred to my modest bank account.

At my debut I played the Lalo *Symphonie espagnole* and the Elgar concerto, with the orchestra performing a Haydn symphony in the interlude between my efforts. The response of the public and the press was gratifying. Unfortunately the original program, press reviews, and other memorabilia pertaining to this event and to this period were destroyed toward the end of World War II. Very often the skillful defense employed in London against the V-1 bombs was to send the Spitfires up to tip over the bombs by flipping the V-1 fins from underneath with the wing tip of the airplane, an intrepid pastime, I am persuaded. As occasionally happened, the bomb, instead of falling out of control to the ground, simply changed course. One day my mother heard the raucous noise of a V-bomb pass overhead, fade into the distance, and then return. Instinct told her to get everyone down into the basement. The house was subsequently flattened and all the family archives destroyed excepting father's billiards table. The family were the only survivors; they were under the billiards table.

Although my actual study on the violin during those four years at Guildhall was not fruitful, the cultural climate of London contributed vitally toward my education. London was a marvelous town to my wide-eyed innocence. I am aware of how much bewitching charm resides in the memories of old times, but I can't recall ever having experienced a bad summer in London. There must have been one, or perhaps more, because the weather in this world isn't as good as all that and London is usually classed sub-par. In my fond recollection, however, every summer had beauty in residence.

I often wandered in the Mayfair district past the fashionable homes. The French windows were frequently open to summer's dews and perfumes and gentle airs, and quite often someone would be touching the piano, never with a fury of sound, but in keeping with the balminess of the night, while the sounds turned in the zephyr of alluring polyphony. I didn't have money in those days to do much other than to savor such magic, take in a movie and an occasional boxing match at the Blackfriars Ring or the Whitechapel Wonderland, where one could see a man get a bloody nose for not more than a couple of "bob." I attended all the galleries and visited the British Museum reading room with other impecunious students and searchers after truth.

The Guildhall School distributed free tickets to concerts, and many of them were on my schedule. Heifetz made his debut in London about this time, playing the Elgar concerto, with Elgar conducting. I remember vividly his recital at the Albert Hall about a week later, when he played, among other things, the Scottish Fantasy of Max Bruch in stupendous fashion. Shortly thereafter came another Russian, Toscha Seidel, from the same Auer source. Here was a dramatic test of position; among ourselves we students were very outspoken and opinionated, as most students are. Not one of us for a moment suggested that Seidel was a better fiddle player than Heifetz, but we pondered whether, if Seidel had appeared first in London, would he or would he not have had the greater *réclame*. He made a notable debut, but he did not have a big audience, he did not have repeat appearances, and he did not return to England for some time.

Several other string players made a deep impression on me while I was a student. I heard Casals for the first time in London when he performed the Lalo concerto, and in the second movement his playing of the lilting middle section literally lifted me out of my seat. I was utterly transported by the ravishing euphoria he induced. When he played the C major suite of Bach, I heard him do something I have never heard before, and I have adapted it to my own use. Where that impressive dignity descends through two octaves to the open C string, as he bowed the last note, Casals plucked the string with his left hand to make sure he gave a clean articulation of the note. That impressed me as being a very sensible and practical thing to do, and especially when I came to play the viola I made use of the device. The viola, being a more recalcitrant instrument than the violin, sometimes needs a *very discreet* amount of left-hand pizzicato to cause the notes to speak with clarity and definition. That is why I adhere to the theory that, on the viola at least, the fingers should not be lifted straight up from the strings, but should come off at a slight angle, yielding an exiguous left-hand pizzicato effect.

I shall never forget a concert, about this same time, in which Casals shared the program with the Czech violinist Váša Příhoda at that monstrous barn, the Albert Hall. Although Příhoda had had a fair amount of publicity and his records were known, the management may have felt that he probably couldn't fill the hall on his own or sustain enough interest for an entire recital. So they added Casals, a strange miscalculation. Mr. Příhoda executed the first half of the program, exposing himself and his astonishing technique in a mess of meretricious music. Mr. Casals then played the second half of the concert.

There was Příhoda in diffident fashion, deploying extremely difficult passages all over the fingerboard, some of them really too banal for public exposure but intended no doubt to make the eyes of the listening string players pop out of their heads. The eyes didn't pop far, however. Příhoda's technique, in contrast to Heifetz's, was pedestrian. It never soared aloft. After so much scampering through a lot of double harmonics, tenths, and sixths, I felt inclined to say, "So what?" Casals followed with unaccompanied Bach!

An old Spanish aficionado attended all of Casals's concerts and consistently perched himself in the front row. He was obviously disgusted and indignant during the Příhoda presentation, indignant that he should be in the same hall, let alone on the same program, with Casals. When Casals came on, the old boy cheered, "Ole! Bravo!" and banged on the floor with his walking stick. That afternoon was indeed memorable.

Kreisler, whom I had heard even earlier in my youth, probably had more influence on me than anybody. His impact was exceedingly strong and has remained powerful and enduring. I include here a story that illustrates his influence and causes some listeners to whom I relate it to regard me as inordinately conceited, which I am not. It is necessary for me to mention first something that was told to me years later by Warwick Evans, cellist of the London String Quartet and a close friend of Kreisler. It seems Kreisler had told him that if Evans ever heard him play a radio program he would know that he, Kreisler, was nearing the end of his career. At that time radio had become an ominous threat to live music (to say nothing of the printed news media) and certain managers cautioned artists that they would get no engagements if they succumbed to the lure of radio. Kreisler and Rachmaninoff made a pact that they would never perform for this medium. (Incidentally, when Kreisler later finally did play for the Bell Telephone Hour he was well on the down side of his career.)

At any rate, at one particular time the BBC ran a nightly series of half-hour programs called the "Foundations of Music," in which one artist devoted one week to the works of one composer. I, for example, played Corelli sonatas and later the unaccompanied sonatas and partitas by Bach. Then I got it into my mind that I would like to play a week of Kreisler transcriptions. I went to Kenneth Wright, who at that time was head of the music department at the BBC, and said, "Look, Ken, these pieces are a wonderful addition to the repertoire of violinists. It is a very significant thing that Kreisler has done for violin literature and for violinists." I argued so eloquently and with such conviction that I eventually persuaded—perhaps coerced—Wright to let me have my way and my week performing the Kreisler *charmeurs*.

What happened, as Warwick Evans told me much later when I was a member of the London String Quartet, was that he tuned in by chance one evening to one of my broadcasts. He called to his wife in great excitement and astonishment, "Come here and listen, quickly. Fritz is playing!" I have previously entered a plea of *nolo contendere* on the charge of conceit, and a prosecutor might further contend that to imitate argues nothing in my favor, except for that particular ability, and I would agree. But the ability to imitate can stand one in very good stead. I play golf well when I play with someone much better than myself. I start to sense his swing and coordinate with his rhythm. When I studied with Ysaÿe, he presented a certain bowing exercise to all of his students. I got it right away just by observing and imitating; others had to spend a good deal of awkward time achieving the same result. At least, because of my particular ability, I was able to mislead Warwick Evans, which indicates the kind of influence Kreisler had on me.

I heard many singers while in London, among them Chaliapin and Galli-Curci, and went to a fair amount of opera, although I have never been an opera buff. I suppose I resented opera because we were obliged to go. The school not only forced us, but gave us free seats. And a Scotsman would attend any event, any entertainment, his own funeral, given a free seat. I favored Strauss, Puccini, and Ravel operas, but I had little patience with the pomposities of *The Ring*. The story and libretto struck me as abysmal and stuffed with Nietzschean philosophy. I very often dozed during the Wagnerian *longueurs,* woke up and identified the *leitmotiv,* and went back to sleep. I did enjoy *The Flying Dutchman,* with its good story, snappy action, and jolly music.

During those young years in London I made some strong and lasting friendships. I had very good times with at least three fellows: Albert Sammons, the violinist; Solomon, the pianist; and Osmond Raphael, a business executive. Osmond was ten years older than I. He and his wife, Kirsty, remained my closest friends until his death. An amateur violinist who also studied at the Guildhall School of Music with Mossel and who was well educated, Osmond came from a distinguished and wealthy family, his father being an alderman of the City of London. I looked forward to each visit at the imposing family home just outside London. Osmond's influence on me was forceful and effective. He perceived the gauche and socially untutored youngster from Glasgow with small knowledge of the world of elegance and the refinements of living. He saw to it that I learned how to dress and behave properly, which fork and knife to use when sitting at a fashionable table, and how important it was to be just as fastidious in a Lyon's teashop as when dining with the *haut monde.* I felt his influence mostly in the "frills" of living, in things generally to do with culture, but slightly on the superficial level, though Osmond was not a superficial person. In certain circumstances these frills, these apparent superficialities, can profoundly influence a person in his attainment of a poised and balanced character.

There were three brothers in the Raphael family, all possessing an acute sense of humor and the absurd. One, Geoffrey, after many successful years as a barrister and K.C. (King's Counsel) eventually sat on the bench at Marylebone Police Court, an important judgeship and a prestigious court among police courts. He became interested in painting as a hobby and justified his choice of pastime. One day he dropped into a colorist's near the court and ordered some paints. When the shopkeeper asked, "Where shall I send

33

Osmond P. Raphael, Primrose's mentor in etiquette

them?" he answered, "Send them to Judge Raphael at Marylebone Police Court." The shopkeeper, perceiving an opening for a quip, asked again, "Any relation to Raphael the artist?" to which my friend responded, "Sir, I *am* Raphael the artist!"

Several unforgettable incidents are associated with my friend Solomon, the pianist. In the south side of London was an ancient theater of no great repute called the "Elephant and Castle," revived in an active way by an actor-manager who rejoiced in the extraordinary name of Tod Slaughter. He restored to the boards old Victorian melodramas such as "Sweeney Todd, the Demon Barber," "East Lynne," and various other tear-jerker "mellers."

It became a venture in fashionable slumming for people from the West End of London to cross to the south bank to attend these plays. They were presented in a most unusual manner—not extraordinary—but in the only manner they could be produced at the modest prices they called for and within Slaughter's economy of means. For instance, I recall in one play a scene depicting a Brigade of Guards' mess, the Coldstream, if you like. Slaughter recruited the bit players from the street, had them dress in Guard's uniform, walk on, sit down at the table to eat an imaginary meal—poor starving, shivering souls—and, after the principals had carried on the conversation, leave. It was at once hilarious and pitiable to see some old fellow with a careworn face, receding chin, and untrimmed walrus mustache, decked out in the uniform of the Brigade of Guards, the fringe of his own ragged pants in evidence underneath, along with his unpolished and cracked boots. Any remaining illusion was destroyed, and few, if any, took these plays seriously.

But I must say that Tod Slaughter and his motley crew began attracting the crowds, and Solomon, other friends, and I often took the stage box for a very modest outlay. Solomon, apart from being one of the world's greatest piano virtuosos, was also one of the world's greatest tin whistlers. He played this humble instrument magnificently and with great virtuosity. The orchestra in the theater pit was composed of a fiddle, clarinet, trumpet, double bass, and a conductor who directed from a battered upright. During one of the entr'actes Solomon sat on the floor of the box where he couldn't be seen and started to play his tin whistle—the apparent flute part of the overture. The poor, bemused pianist-conductor kept looking around his orchestra to see where this magic flute playing was coming from. He never did find out.

That was just one of our escapades. Another one took place when Solomon, with his swarthy face and jet black hair, bought himself a false beard—a full beard of Titian red. He put it on at one performance during a very sentimental scene, got up on his knees on the edge of the box, and leaned over as far as he safely could, in proximity with the stage. The actress, engaged in a scene of passion and pathos, caught sight of him, took one look, and flew into a panic and blew her lines.

The stage box became notorious and we drew our own personal applause from the audience, particularly from the cockneys up in the "gods," the gallery. We became so much a part of the show that finally Tod Slaughter sent for us to come down to his dressing room, where we drank beer with him. He was highly grateful and adjured us to attend as often as we could, as it was "just dandy for the box office." In the years following my departure for the United States I spent very little time in London, and my friendship with Solomon faded from lack of a common contact. Then there was his lamentable illness. I have not seen him for many years.

To many, my other confrere, Albert Sammons, was the ranking British violinist of his time. He was also a great boxing fan, as were Solomon and, of course, myself. As a matter of fact, Albert had also done a little bit of sparring as an amateur. I remember him for his charming off-cockney accent. On one occasion Solomon and I attended one of the weekly fights at the Albert Hall and that evening a British champion, for reasons unknown to man, beat an American. As the American went plunk on the floor, Albert, who was sitting behind us and well aware that on the previous Sunday Elman, Heifetz, or Kreisler might have performed in the same arena, leaned over between us and said, "What a tone!"

Albert could have had a career of high import. He was the original first violinist of the London String Quartet and was succeeded by James Levey, the latter subsequently known throughout the United States through his leadership of the group. Albert, on the other hand, was scarcely known at all, except to a few musicians, as he never ventured any further afield than Dieppe, France—a one-hour trip across the channel. He was a violinist of the highest rank and more or less self-taught. Eventually he became Beecham's concertmaster at Covent Garden before venturing forth as soloist, though restricting himself to a parochial field of action. A friend of his once said that Albert's telegraphic address should be "The Village Pump, London." He had a pleasant home in the country, a modest one, and liked to play golf and live a quiet life.

When the London String Quartet performed in the States shortly after the First World War, their manager—I think his name was

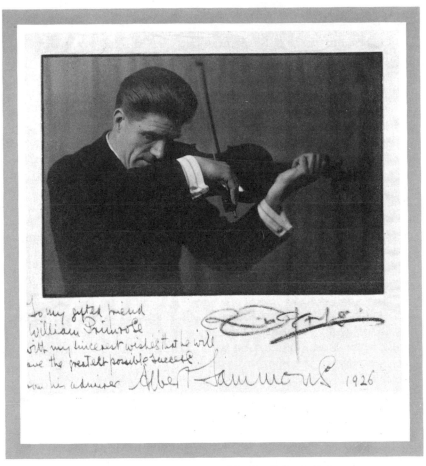

To my gifted friend
William Primrose
with my sincerest wishes that he will
have the greatest possible success
from his admirer Albert Sammons 1926

Albert Sammons, notable English violinist

Adams—was looking around for a foil to Heifetz. He wanted to introduce another foreign violinist other than a Russian because he felt it would make very good business for all concerned. He discussed the scheme with Levey and Warwick Evans and inquired if anyone in England could fit the bill. They very warmly and strongly recommended Albert Sammons, and preparations were made for him to come. When the quartet returned to England they inquired of Albert, "When do you leave for the States?"

He answered that he was not going.

"You're not going? But we don't understand. You have a marvelous chance, a marvelous entrée for your first tour. You're not going to make a fortune this time, but you will the next. And you won't *lose* any money."

"No, I'm not going," he protested. "They'd start comparing me with Heifetz and Elman."

You see, he had a small-town—a parochial—mind. A monstrous pity, for he was a great violinist.

I believe Albert could have held his own against the Auer-prodigies. I don't recall hearing him play anything that showed off transcendental or flashy technique. But I did hear him play very vividly such works as the Beethoven, Elgar, and Delius concertos, Bach, and a lot of chamber music. He had only one fault in my opinion, and other outstanding violinists have the same failing: he vibrated too much. He vibrated on every note, and sometimes the intensity became overpowering to my ears. Nevertheless he possessed a beautiful tone and all the technique requisite to performing the works I heard him play. Elgar, after all, isn't too easy a concerto to play technically, left hand or right. Albert had the makings, but not "what it takes"—what my Jewish friends call *chutzpah*: gall. By the time I had walked the Damascus road, seen the light, repented of past transgressions, and turned to the viola, I frequently engaged in concerts with the BBC Orchestra. After one of these performances, when I returned to the artist's room, I became aware of a frail, bent figure trembling from head to foot with Parkinson's disease. He said, "Hello, Bill," and I saw that it was Albert Sammons, the Albert who in his day had been a handsome, well-favored man, athletic and debonair.

One thing I believe hurt Albert's *amour propre* more than anything else. After Kreisler's initial performance Albert was the first person to play the Elgar concerto extensively. He was never asked to record it, however, although Heifetz and Menuhin were, and he remained very bitter about it. Albert subscribed to the old shibboleth that if you don't have a foreign name you are never going to be accepted by a British audience. This was true to a certain extent, and thereby hangs a hilarious story.

There was, eons ago, an English violinist by the name of John Dunn. My father told me he was an exceptional player and a complete eccentric. He did the most incomprehensible things. For instance, on one particular day after morning rehearsal, he proceeded to take an invigorating country constitutional, returning for the concert in the afternoon. He had *definitely* been out in the country in the fields and in the ditches, encountering all manner of bucolic obstacles; and when he came back, his shoes were covered with mud and ancillary detritus. He was just about to go on stage, undisturbed in any way, when the manager caught full sight of him and, horrified, forbade him to appear as he was, with particular reference to his footwear. So he took off his shoes and played in his stocking feet.

There are a great many stories about Dunn, some of them apocryphal, to be sure. He disappeared from public scrutiny for a while, and then suddenly a violinist by the name of Ivan Donovitch presented himself to the London public. This was of course none other than John Dunn. He thought a more exotic name would get him further, but his deception was readily discovered and his hopes foundered.

There seems always to be a particular appeal in the charm of the unfamiliar, be it a name, a face, or a mannerism. In America and especially in Great Britain a foreign name has the feel of something new and strange. I remember from my student days in London that the most exotic thing about Heifetz, apart from his playing, was his magnificent head of hair, always combed pompadour. Toscha Seidel aped the same style, as did many of our native fiddlers, but this didn't help their playing to any appreciable extent that I recall.

Primrose in London at age 22

4

Warming Up

In 1924 my toil at the Guildhall School of Music finally came to an end. I was given a gold medal, the highest award that is offered each year, and had my name inscribed in the main hall of the school among others from the nineteenth century onward who had won the same recognition. Later I was made "Fellow" of the school, which is the significance of the "F.G.S.M." that sometimes accompanies my name.

I then began playing a large number of concerts and doing a lot of broadcasting; but frankly my career was badly handled. There was no plan, no one to guide me along the path that leads to success. Now the whole conception of management has changed. In my salad days a management, with some rare exceptions—Lionel Powell in London and sundry others like him in the States—was little more than a booking agency. Booking agents didn't "promote"; they did not conceive of this as being part of their business. The artist was constrained to promote himself as best he knew how. He bought space in the columns of the Saturday edition of the London *Daily Telegraph,* for instance, in which announcements of the forthcoming week's concerts were published, and displayed his recent reviews—the favorable ones, of course. The artist trusted that these reviews might impress a local promoter sufficiently to cause him to approach his (the artist's) London representative with the offer of an engagement. During an artist's early days this was a thankless and frustrating experience.

The broadcasting studios were primitive by present-day standards. One of the problems was the echo. To offset this destructive element, the studios were draped in the manner of an oriental harem. When I first tried to play against this dampening down of the tone, it was a calamity, disturbing to the point of irritation. But one simply had to get used to it. Along with the London station were regional stations. An artist would be engaged to play in London; then Birmingham, Newcastle, Manchester, Edinburgh, Aberdeen, and Glasgow; over in Belfast and Dublin; back through Cardiff; and so on. These tours were fairly lucrative, and, once the trick of playing amid the draperies was mastered, very pleasant for a young, struggling, and perchance impecunious artist. Then too he was in the studio and free of the usual strain of playing in public. If he didn't feel like memorizing a piece, he might use the music. For me, this congenial state of affairs lasted only till the advent of the "national" hook-up, distinct of course from the "regional."

My first recording for His Master's Voice was the Saint-Saëns Introduction and Rondo Capriccioso with piano.* That was in the days before electrical recording, when a huge apparatus that looked like an old-fashioned gramophone horn was sticking out of the wall. The artist would tilt his instrument toward it and play into it for four and a half minutes, with the hope that when he untilted his instrument he would have recorded some four and a half minutes of passable performance. I inscribed the Bach A major sonata with piano and a few other works, but even this branch of my activity was fraught with mismanagement and failed for my lack of wise advice. As we shall see, my HMV (His Master's Voice) contract expired and was not renewed, but this was actually a fortunate contingency. Shortly afterward I signed a contract with English Columbia.

---

*Recently an ardent collector in New York graciously sent me a cassette reproduction of this venerable disc, which I had not heard in many years. It was a charming and touching experience to listen to this recording, made fifty-four years ago!

Recording companies then were accustomed to paying advance royalties, and Columbia paid me one hundred pounds, which was impressive to me in my then precarious fiscal condition. I sensed later that I hadn't earned that much in sales or anything approaching it. Some years afterward, when I had become entirely involved with the viola and had the fifth, the thirteenth, and other Paganini caprices up my sleeve as a sort of blockbuster, I went to Arthur Brooks, Columbia's recording manager, and told him I would like to make viola records. He replied, "Please don't ask me to do that. I'll lose my job." They had been recording a very distinguished violist for some time, with an unfortunate financial return.

At this I ventured, "Arthur, do you remember that you paid me a hundred pounds advance royalties for violin recordings a few years ago?"

"Indeed, I do," was his rueful retort.

"Well," I went on, "go get the books and let's see how much on that account I have actually earned."

The ledger forthcoming, we found that I had earned about half of the advance. And so I proposed that he allow me to record two of the Paganini caprices on the viola at the cost of overhead alone. I guaranteed to do them in only one morning session and he was not to pay me a penny until the balance of the advance was amortized. He agreed, and I recorded the Paganini caprices. As a result my career on the viola was aided immensely. I have frequently pondered whether I could have sold Columbia on the idea of recording the viola had the violin recordings been more successful from the sales standpoint.

At first, broadcasting was in sundry ways the most demanding kind of performing I did. It took me a while to get used to playing for a public I could not see. As I have already mentioned, the studios themselves were very disconcerting. Through the years, however, I came to do a good deal of broadcasting, both on the violin and the viola.

It was tremendously fortunate that the BBC was in full control of broadcasting in Great Britain at that time, because the standards it set were exalted. John Reith, later Sir John and eventually Lord Reith, a man of almost Calvinistic purity and ideals, was head of the corporation, and he imposed his ideals on the listening public. He was consequently bitterly opposed by a sector of that public and by most of the newspapers. But he stuck by his standards. Under his auspices one heard only the greatest music from the channel presenting this type of program. Other channels were devoted to lighter fare, but always in good taste. The BBC Orchestra was eventually formed, in time becoming one of the most highly esteemed orchestras in Europe.

An amusing story is attached to the BBC broadcasts of the Bach cantatas. These imposing works of monumental musical importance, albeit occasionally tedious, were broadcast every Sunday afternoon over a period of years. To a sector of the public they became anathema, even notorious. As the story goes, a friend of mine, a bass player, had been out of town to fulfill an engagement and had traveled all night by train back to London to return in time for the broadcast. Arriving Sunday morning, he jumped into a taxi and asked the driver to take him to Broadcasting House as quickly as possible, as he had to make the morning rehearsal. During the drive from Euston Station, the taxi driver, eyeing the bulky instrument, asked suspiciously, "You play bass?"

My friend admitted to playing bass.

"What's the program you're hurrying to?" the driver further enquired.

My friend replied, "I'm doing the Bach cantata program."

"Bach what?" the driver asked.

"Cantata," said my friend.

And the driver exploded with, "Then you can bloody well get out and walk!"

Reith's standards were indeed eminent. I don't believe he was a musician in any sense at all, but he left it to his music department to fulfill his vision. He believed in the department, trusted it, and supported it. The people in charge were highly intelligent and in most cases not merely business executives but themselves musicians of some stature. Broadcasting became a most pleasurable activity for me because I could perform a lofty standard of music. When I was touring and performing regular programs in the smaller provincial towns, I had frequently to play down a bit to "temper the wind to the shorn lamb." So a program for the BBC constituted a balm and a solace.

Difficulties were compounded in the days of recording on 78 rpm because we had to make approximately four and one-half minutes of perfect or near-perfect recording per side. On top of that we had to thrust ourselves acrobatically into this apparatus that stuck out of the wall, which I have already described. I was engaged by HMV when the company was experimenting with the original long-playing records, many years before they became marketable. I was asked to record once more the Rondo Capriccioso, which lasts some ten minutes. This was recorded on one side, a thing unheard of in those days. Those particular experiments were unsuccessful and the recordings were never released. But I had actually taken part in the pioneer experience.

Always intervening in my broadcasting and recording activities as a violinist was my desire to become a violist. My father owned a very beautiful viola—a Brothers Amati. As a youngster, when he wasn't around, I found a way to open the latch on the cupboard where the Amati was kept and played it with considerable satisfaction. I preferred its sound to that of the violin. The only serious thought I might have given to a career as a violist at that point, however, was coupled with my intense desire to take part in chamber music. I had enough knowledge of the situation to know that there was a dearth of really good viola players. I thought someday a string quartet might ask me to fulfill the role of violist. If so I would be ready. I would know how to read the clef and know the technique of the instrument.

Certainly many of the subtleties of playing the viola were foreign to me at that time. I approached the task as so many people did and still do, endeavoring to solve problems as if I were performing on an oversized violin, which is quite the wrong approach. Now I don't wish to denigrate my abilities as a violinist. As a matter of fact I always had the London String Quartet in mind because it was the greatest quartet from my homeland and vying for the top spot in world esteem with the Flonzaley. But I was aware that the violinists playing in it at the time were very unlikely to leave the group. Perhaps I was being too Scots about the whole thing, too canny and calculating, while awaiting the proverbial knock on the door, which we are told is the habit opportunity persists in and in which it so often goes unheeded.

My early concertizing by force of circumstance was almost exclusively limited to the United Kingdom. Not that I was in the least like Sammons. I wasn't. I lusted after the adventure of travel. I did make an appearance in Paris in 1928, however, playing the Mozart concertante with Lionel Tertis, the violist, and with Beecham conducting. By this time I had definitely made up my mind to switch to viola, but I didn't tell anyone. I'm reasonably sure, though, that if I had advised Tertis of my secret ambition he would have welcomed me with open arms, because he was *the* great viola protagonist. As my decision finally became known, some people were aghast and my father deeply despondent. When I had at last burned my bridges, one individual, a very distinguished orchestra player and highly respected, told me, "You're making the biggest mistake of your life. You will regret this as you've regretted no other thing." I wonder what he thinks now.

Shortly before I crossed the Rubicon, I undertook an exceedingly interesting tour in East Africa. Percy Hemming, a very popular singer at Covent Garden, and I were engaged by the wife of an American businessman, who organized a series of concerts in every conceivable community in Kenya and Uganda. She was an ardent music lover and went to incredible lengths to make her venture a success, with no thought of financial gain. Often there was no auditorium, not even a schoolhouse, and we would perform in somebody's drawing room. Quite a number of the people were very wealthy planters who had palatial homes, invariably referred to as "bungalows."

The whole trip, following at a few days' interval the trek of the Martin Johnsons, was a never-ending revelation of the extraordinary and the incredible. For example, we gave a concert at a place called Jinja, located close to the source of the Nile. It has the only golf course in the world I know of where if one's ball lands in the footprint of a hippopotamus he can pick it up and set it down on a more negotiable lie without losing a stroke—which is only equitable, as the hippos come up during the night from Lake Victoria and wander all over the place. We took an impressive trip across a mountain range and descending into the Great Rift Valley, my eyes were met with phantasm. As we approached Lake Nakuru, I remarked to our hostess and manager, "Well, that's really a first! Pink sand."

"That's not sand," she said. "Those are flamingoes." So closely packed together they were that from the distance they had the solid appearance of sand.

At the source of the Nile itself, as I was putting my hand into the water to test the temperature, an object close to the bank, which I took to be a log, suddenly came to life, its great jaws widening before me. I hardly need add that I beat a hasty retreat from that place. We traveled mostly by car that was covered with heavy netting to keep out the tsetse flies and other pests that converged upon us as we motored through the jungle. I finished the tour with a case of malaria, which persisted for several years and was an interesting memento of the expedition, to say the least.

Such fascinating events and equally interesting personalities come easily to my memory. Benno Moiseiwitch, the pianist, and I were both members of the Savage Club in London, and we frequently performed together at the house dinners, to our mutual satisfaction, I believe. The remarkable thing about him, besides his transcendental pianism, was the sphinxlike mask he assumed in public and when playing poker. To paraphrase Erskine Childers: "If ever I saw a straight flush under a mask..." No matter what happened or what he was playing, piano or cards (he was a rigorous and heavy gambler and a brilliant card player), the face never changed. It was the epitome of understatement and reserve, with the eyelids lowered, the mouth slightly pursed and turned down at the corners. He never smiled, never altered his features at all. Facial architecture? Perhaps his "next of kin" in this conceit was Rachmaninoff, and the two of them were on the coldest terms of warm friendship.

The Savage Club itself is worth describing. The only thing comparable to it in the United States that I am aware of, and to which I belonged, is the Players Club in New York, founded by the actor Edwin Booth, brother of Lincoln's assassin. The membership of the Savage Club was limited to people who earned their living from the arts, sometimes indirectly, such as a few prominent surgeons and other Harley Street specialists who qualified for membership by having written notable treatises on their respective subjects.

The membership ranged from very wealthy theatrical producers to the seediest out-of-work actor in the business and ran the same gamut in the other arts. The club had an excellent cuisine, not expensive, and the annual dues were not excessive; so the involuntary penny-pinchers could scrape home. When I first joined, the premises were in Adelphi Terrace and we had such neighbors as George Bernard Shaw and Sir James Barrie. The gracious old houses overlooked the Thames, but later were cruelly and thoughtlessly demolished to make way for an office building. We moved to premises in Carlton House Terrace, not far from the German Embassy, an ignoble neighbor to have in those Ribbentrop days.

The Savage Club was in many ways a plebeian outfit, replete with characters, one of whom was an old blackguard known as "Old O'Dell." He had been an actor of sorts during the latter part of the nineteenth century. He possessed a mordant and viperish wit and made such a sinister impression on the membership of the club that even to this day, years after his death, a brass plaque still memorializes "his" chair: "Here sat Old O'Dell." And woe betide the scrub member who would dare to sit there uninvited! On one memorable occasion Old O'Dell ordered King George VI out of his chair when the King, then Duke of York, was a guest. HRH, highly amused, abdicated O'Dell's throne.

Primrose later as a mature artist, in rehearsal

The old fellow had a high, quavering voice, sported Dundreary whiskers, an actor's cape, and a large, umbraceous sombrero. His ploy was to lure new members into lending him money (he was constantly hard up) and he was not infrequently successful. He could impress a novitiate with his malign dignity and make a fledgling member feel as though he, O'Dell, owned the club and all the rights thereto. One fine day one young fellow found himself in need of some money to pay for drinks. He spotted Old O'Dell in his favorite chair near the bar, where he was most likely to curry a few complimentary libations, approached him, and said, "Do you mind, O'Dell. You remember the five pounds I lent you last year? May I have it back?"

O'Dell replied, "Young man, I haven't finished with it yet!"

We had rare entertainment at the Savage Club. Moiseiwitch played often, as did Mark Hambourg, and I did a bit of fiddling myself with Benno, as I remarked earlier. Many visiting artists, such as Rachmaninoff and other distinguished guests, performed there, not to mention a host of equally distinguished members—a galaxy of talent to make any impresario drool.

I played with a great many accompaniments in those days, both good and bad. My first recording for RCA—the Brahms E-flat sonata—was made in London with Gerald Moore. I had known Gerald when he was an aspiring solo pianist and hadn't yet attained the fame that was to come to him—and was due him—as an accompanist. When I first played in England and was still quite young, the fees weren't remarkable for "locals" like myself and didn't allow for engaging a permanent accompanist. Moreover it would have been looked upon as presumptuous for a native son to engage a permanent accompanist such as a bigwig from abroad.

Almost always I had to "suffer" a local pianist, some of whom were unbelievably bad. Some, aware of their inadequacies, were only crestfallen, and others quite oblivious. I encountered one of these latter gentry in a small town in northern England. He looked as if he was a man who enjoyed his toddy, rather corpulent and jolly, with red face and bristling mustache. I was playing a not too demanding program—probably a Handel sonata, maybe a minor violin concerto, and a group of Kreisler transcriptions. My accompanist could not negotiate any of these, but this did not perturb him in the least. He could see that it was perturbing me, however, and in an effort to put me at ease he said, "Don't worry about tonight, lad, you just play your part, and I'll keep busy in the key."

He approximated to this comforting pledge. And I must confess he had a very quick ear. He seldom digressed into the wrong key; and when he did, he very promptly got back into the right one. It was a hilarious concert. Such are the rewards—or hazards—of the performing artist.

Eugène Ysaÿe, whose advice was prophetic

5

Ysaÿe

Though my association with my teacher in London was rather unfortunate, I am quite prepared to believe that some of the misfortune was of my own making. I think he was not very involved in teaching and I was not very interested in the few things he had to tell me. Nothing prompted me to practice. I lacked motivation.

I was also becoming quite aware that I was beginning to go downhill as a player. Fortunately a very good friend of mine at the time, Ivor Newton, one of the most prestigious accompanists in England, offered me some much-needed advice. He accompanied for most of the great artists of his time, including Ysaÿe. On occasion he also played for William Primrose and took a flattering interest in my career.

One day Newton said, "I have to be frank with you and tell you that your playing is going off." I answered that I knew it, but I simply had no interest, no inspiration. He said, "Why don't you go abroad and study, perhaps with Ysaÿe?" He had already talked to

Ysaÿe about me and suggested that I write him, which I did. I received a letter from Ysaÿe's amanuensis, who eventually became his second wife, saying that Le Maître would be glad to accept me as a student. She named the fee, which was not excessive by our present-day standards but a bit more than I was prepared to pay. However I decided to sign up with Ysaÿe first and then solve my money problem.

I was able to negotiate payment for my lessons quite literally by chance. A few days after I enrolled with Le Maître at his summer residence at Le Zoute Sur Mer, I took a day off. Now I must confess that I am a very poor gambler. I have no card sense to speak of; and when it comes to games of chance, everything seems to go against me. I had never seen a roulette wheel. At a nearby resort named Blankenbergh there was a fashionable casino, and at the "pension" where I was lodging were some young holiday-makers who planned to pay a visit to the casino for a little flutter. They invited me to join them and I went along. Though I knew nothing about the game of roulette, I did see that there were certain hazards named "pair" and "impair," even and odd numbers, which reduced the choice of hazards to the minimum of calculation. In my innocence I put the chip on the "impair," the odd number, and won. It was just as we so often read in many improbable tales where the lucky person leaves his chips and forgets. As I remember it now I always recall with laughter, holding both sides, Somerset Maugham's *Boutade*. I left my money and my lucky number came up about ten times in succession—and won a colossal fortune! At least it was so by my standard.

Hard-bitten gamblers were standing around watching me. My original stake had been the smallest acceptable, but I had won approximately 250 pounds, at that time about the equivalent of $1,250—enough to pay my fees to Ysaÿe for the summer. The fall and winter obligations would look out for themselves! That was my only positive encounter with good fortune. She never patted me on the head again. A few years ago I motored to the west coast and spent an evening in Las Vegas. I decided to again visit a casino, thinking that I would repeat the experience of so long ago: I would of course put my stake on "impair." But when I reached the casino and the table, somebody was standing in the way and I couldn't reach over to place my stake. I put my stake on the even number and lost. That ended my gambling career. *Faute de mieux*.

Beginning in 1926 I studied with Ysaÿe on and off for about three years, mostly in the summers and the occasional winters. I had certain reservations about studying with him at first because he was then toward the end of his concert career and was not performing at all well in public. He suffered abominably from nerves and it was painfully evident. Of course we all do (only bad players are not nervous), but we keep them under control, as Ysaÿe manifestly did in his prime. The last concert I heard him play, shortly after his wife died, was frankly an unfortunate one. It was at the Albert Hall in London, where the echo is so pronounced that it inspired Beecham to remark that it was the only place a British composer was certain to hear his work twice. Only toward the end of the recital did Ysaÿe come into his own when he played, as only he could play, the Vieuxtemps Ballade and Polonaise, and gave the startlingly brilliant performance we had been used to in the past. The rest of the concert was acutely sad. However, after I went to him as a student, my apprehension was quickly dispelled, for in private he played just as beautifully and nobly as he had always done.

Ysaÿe was a unique figure in every sense of the word and profoundly engaging. He was a big man in appearance and had a heart to match. He was over-generous, and his style of playing was always in the grand manner. Though he was not a pedagogue in the accepted sense of the word, as, for instance, we think of Flesch or Ševčik, he exerted great influence on his students. I commented earlier that I have the ability quickly and accurately to imitate, which can be either a drawback or an advantage. Consequently, just by hearkening to Ysaÿe's demonstration I was able to do things the way he advised without too much difficulty.

He was an enduring inspiration. In the accompaniments he devised for the concertos I prepared for him, he played on his own violin, in quite astonishing fashion, all the harmonies and counterpoint of the score (to say nothing of his implications of the orchestration), appearing to reproduce all this with surprising felicity. For him everything in the matter or tone resided in one word, which he used repeatedly: *sonorité, toujours la sonorité.*

Ysaÿe was a man of vast erudition. In his copy of the Bach violin and cello suites that are published together in one volume in the *Gesellschaft* edition, he had inscribed quotations from Rousseau above each movement, quotations that he felt were apt to the spirit which informed them. And thereby hangs a tale of misunderstanding, misfortune, and whimsy.

This volume gave rise to an incident that evoked another side of Ysaÿe I hadn't known existed. In the midst of one of my summer sessions I had to make a hurried return to London for a few days.

53

At the time, I was working on one of the partitas, and Ysaÿe lent me his copy of the *Gesellschaft* edition so that I might copy his fingerings and phrasings, to say nothing of J. J. Rousseau, with all possible dispatch. He had the entire set of some forty-odd volumes beautifully bound in vellum and hand tooled. I sailed from Ostend to Dover on a very rough day and I handed my suitcase, which contained Ysaÿe's precious volume, to a porter at Ostend, who put it, or so I believed, with the other baggage on deck. About halfway across I had cause to look for my case and couldn't find it. More than a trifle concerned, I reported the loss to the captain, who sent a wireless to the police at Dover.

When we docked, I was instructed to stand on the bridge and observe the passengers debark. If I spotted anyone with my case, I was commanded to point him out to a couple of plainclothesmen on the gangplank. Everyone got off, but I failed to spot the suitcase or the conjectured thief. We then looked for it on board, but to no avail. I didn't mind losing anything else, but my heart sank at the loss of Ysaÿe's music. As soon as I could, I went to a music store in London and bought a recent issue of the *Gesellschaft* volume—not the same year of publication, of course, and certainly not with the markings or the luxurious binding of Ysaÿe's copy. However I thought it was better than nothing and would serve as a token of my deep chagrin.

Returning to Belgium a few days later, I attempted to tell Ysaÿe what had transpired. At first he seemed to take it perfectly well, to display an authentic British sangfroid, but apparently that was because he didn't understand completely what I was trying to convey. I then proceeded to make it very clear to him and that was when he gave way to fury, although not so much at me personally, or so I conjectured, but at malign fate. This was a major disaster for him—the loss of one volume from a set which could never be replaced. He might have taken the one I offered in its place, secure that he could recall all that he had written—the legends from Rousseau, his fingerings and bowings—and he could have replaced the binding. But this, of course, would not have been the same. The volume was irreplaceable. Soon, however, he had his anger under control and the status quo was restored.

The incident in full was not yet over, however. A few months later I was appearing as soloist with the Hallé Orchestra in Manchester, at the time Sir Hamilton Harty was the conductor. After rehearsal I went back to the hotel for lunch and was called to the telephone, a long-distance call from London, an exceptional thing in those days for anyone other than a business tycoon or an ambassador. It was Scotland Yard. They had pursued my loss during all the intervening months and had traced the case to Ostend. It had never been put on board; and though it had been rifled, the only things extracted were an Agfa camera and some silk ties. The Ysaÿe *Gesellschaft* copy remained inviolate.

With exceeding glee and to his delight, I returned Ysaÿe's treasure to him. I remember the situation of the loss as being the only time I caught him off emotional balance, so to speak. Otherwise he was most wonderfully generous, most kindly disposed.

Early in my studies with him I was introduced to his own unaccompanied violin sonatas. As a matter of fact I think I played at least one of them in manuscript. After publication performances were exiguous. Later, however, the Russians discovered them—Oistrakh and subsequently Kogan, to name but two. They became the ardent protagonists and propagandists for the compositions.

Along with these sonatas I studied Bach. Ysaÿe was one of those people who could make unaccompanied Bach sound just as I believe it should because of his discriminating ear, sense of sonority, his ability to rescue Bach from the moribund "Victorian Organist" manner of performance, and his very unusual and deftly original fingerings. I got the impression from observing those fingerings and from the way he discussed them in general that he didn't "think" in positions. The whole fingerboard was one position. I find that particularly with the viola this concept is practical and fruitful. I believe that if an artist becomes position-bound, as anyone who becomes muscle-bound, he creates an obstacle to celerity and agility. Speaking of unaccompanied Bach performance, I have come to the conclusion, the result of many painful auditory experiences, that violinists and cellists, like doctors or lawyers, should be licensed before beeing allowed to display their skills, or lack of them, to an unwary public.

There was much for me to learn from Ysaÿe. Even in regard to scales he did not have me approach them in the conventional fashion. There had to be a good reason—and musical, to boot—for such practice. In my book *The Art and Practice of Scale Playing on the Viola* (a Belwin-Mills publication, 1954), I follow almost entirely the method I learned from him for scales practice: for example, I practiced in modulations instead of going, as one usually does, from relative to major to minor. A more comprehensive knowledge of the fingerboard is thus acquired. I reiterate in the preface of my book what Ysaÿe called to my attention—that this is not the *only* way to play scales; rather, it is *another* way.

I adopted most of his fingerings and adapted them in the above-mentioned book for viola: the open strings are used extensively, the lower positions are respected until one *has* to shift higher, and most of the shifts are made on half steps. This last device gave Ysaÿe a generous smoothness. My teacher also introduced to me the phenomenon of the open string sounding an octave above when one descends rapidly. It enables one to leap a whole tone, for example, or two and three positions just by rapidly playing the open string, which sounds the octave above. I had never come across this device before and have found that in certain passages it is indeed an exceptional help.

I was enthralled by Ysaÿe's bowing technique. He was able to extract a superb sonority from the instrument. Szigeti, in his book *Szigeti on the Violin* (London: Cassell, 1969), recalls one of the great moments in Ysaÿe's performance of the ascending scale that immediately precedes the recapitulation in the first movement of the "Spring" Sonata by Beethoven. An F-major scale starts on the G-string and rises in crescendo to a *subito piano,* and the first subject then returns. Ysaÿe drew a phenomenal sound at that juncture with a down bow that never "bumped" across the strings. His bow followed the curve of the bridge. Observe the average violinist, or violist, cross strings, and at the string change a shocking concussion ensues. This is the point that Ysaÿe stressed to his students and Szigeti stresses in his book: *follow the line of the bridge.*

I remember the first time I saw Ysaÿe play—long before I went to study with him. I got the impression, he being such a big man, that he was playing with a bow about the length of an ordinary pencil. He seemed to get from one end of the bow to the other with grace and celerity and played most of his detaché in the upper third, not the middle. I have followed this method since and admonish my students to do the same. The only time I find myself playing toward in the middle is in certain spiccato passages. Sometimes I verge on the facetious and suggest to my students that the middle of the bow is only there to enable them to get from the tip to the frog.

I had had a bowing problem that somewhat vexed me before going to Ysaÿe, but he cleared it up in short order. Part of the antidote lay in the technique of string crossing, which I have described, and part in my observation that Ysaÿe positioned his upper arm low. I had played with a high arm, my elbow tilted up, as became any well-conducted Ševčik student, but this tended to *press* the

56

bow into the strings. Ysaÿe advocated *drawing* the bow across the string, pulling the tone out, and never pressing. I remarked before that he was not a pedagogue in the accepted sense of the word. He did not chatter, but played often. And as he played, I could see the angle of his arm, the height of his elbow, and the trajectory of the bow, and I observed quickly how it was accomplished.

When I listen to Ysaÿe's records today, I sometimes find it difficult to repress a furtive smile as he slides up to a note and slides out of it, a practice perfectly acceptable in his time but now frowned upon. Apart from this mannerism I believe that everybody learned from him, and his house in Brussels became a mecca for all violinists. Kreisler, Elman, Szigeti, Quiroga—the Spanish violinist— were frequent visitors there. Then there were also Ysaÿe's quartet colleagues: Crickboom, Van Hout, and Jacob. I was occasionally invited to his home for dinner and always some distinguished person was present, though not necessarily connected with music: literature, poetry, painting, and, not infrequently, drama graced the board.

It was natural that Ysaÿe should reminisce about his associations with musicians of his time—Wieniawski, Vieuxtemps, Franck, Joachim, and others. I had a feeling that he wasn't very sympathetic toward Joachim, that he did not approve of the German approach to string playing, and I have a fellow feeling with him there because I have little fondness for it myself.

I had one ill-starred lesson with Ysaÿe, and that was indirectly the fault of Gene Tunney, the boxer. I chided Mr. Tunney about it many years later when I met him after a performance of *Harold in Italy,* which I performed with Koussevitsky and the Boston Symphony at Tanglewood. I taught at Tanglewood that entire summer, and at almost every concert I observed Mr. and Mrs. Tunney. Mr. Tunney was a very striking figure (and here no pun is intended, I give you my word), broad shouldered, faultlessly attired in white tuxedo. When I was introduced to him, he was flattering in his observations, and I thought I would make merry with the occasion.

"Mr. Tunney," I opened, "you are the reason I had my only unfortunate lesson with my old master, Ysaÿe." I was impressed that the name evoked no perplexity in Mr. Tunney; he appeared to be fully aware of whom I was speaking and only desired to know why he had been to blame. So I told him that in those days I had a radio that could pick up American stations on short wave—one of the first of its kind. On the night when he fought Dempsey for the second time, most of the students came to my room and we greeted

57

Primrose in 1959

the dawn still listening to the fight, drinking beer rather freely. I had a lesson at nine o'clock in the morning and it was less than successful.

Tunney responded: "Mr. Primrose, you have one consolation: I am the ex-champion and you are still the champion!"

Evenings at Le Zoute were frequently devoted to chamber music. It was at one of these soirees that Ysaÿe suggested I should switch to viola. He seemed to indicate that I had some special aptitude for it. I've often wondered how much that opinion was engendered by a desire to have a violist at hand for his quartet evenings. Most of the students could play viola after a fashion, but perhaps I did have some special flair for it after all. I had been hankering to make the change for some time, but, as I have mentioned, parental opposition was obdurate. Most of my friends, when they learned I was making the change, also thought I was behaving in a foolish and irresponsible manner. They thought it was a form of musical suicide. Having Ysaÿe's approval, however, helped me strengthen my resolve and gave me enough courage to follow my own yearning.*

---

*Ysaÿe is said to have once commented to this effect: "We must not overlook the viola either. This instrument is a necessity in all groups and must not be looked down upon. Both Paganini and Vieuxtemps played the viola from choice, and Joachim loved the color of the bigger instrument. My friend Tertis is doing much missionary work for his viola, and I have had a young man from Scotland who will blaze new paths in the years to come."

The London String Quartet. Top to bottom: Warwick Evans, cello;
John Pennington, 1st violin; William Primrose, viola; and
Thomas Petre, 2nd violin

6

The LS2

My romance with chamber music has been a long one. There were, of course, the wonderful chamber music evenings I indulged in with other students of Ysaÿe. My introduction to quartet playing on a full-time, professional basis, however, came about through rather peculiar circumstances.

Somewhere around 1927 James Levey resigned from the London String Quartet—one of the foremost chamber groups of the day—leaving an opening for a first violinist. This was something I had not anticipated when I was preparing myself to fill a possible viola vacancy, as I mentioned earlier. Warwick Evans, who founded the quartet in 1908, even had me in mind for the violinist's position. He later told me that he had planned to approach me, but while attending a concert one evening he met John Pennington. Pennington was well known in orchestral circles in London and had also formed a quartet of his own—of good repute. He did not have a reputation as a soloist, but John, a very saucy young man at that time, self-assured and not likely to stand on ceremony, approached Mr. Evans and said, "Hello, Evans, I hear you're looking for a fiddle player. Well, you don't have to look any further." Evans, a bit of a cavalier himself, was impressed with John's breezy bravado and, aware of his skill as a violinist, immediately invited him to join the quartet. Needless to say, an invitation so artfully contrived by John was not rejected. But for this fortuitous meeting I would have been the first in line to be considered.

Then in 1930 Waldo Warner, who had been the violist in the quartet since its founding, retired for reasons of health. By this time I had pretty well made up my mind that I was going to be a violist; so when I heard of Warner's resignation I called Evans, arranged to see him, and made the short train journey to his house in the country just outside London. When I explained the reason for the interview, he looked at me and cried, "If I'd only known! If I'd only known! We have engaged someone else." Evans, of course, knew of me as a violinist, but not of my secret aspiration. He mentioned a player fairly well known in orchestral circles and added that this man hadn't wished to join them in the first place because he very much disliked the idea of traveling, let alone the idea of leaving England. "But I urged him into joining," continued Evans, "and I can't ask him to resign now before he's played one concert." He was downcast, and so was I.

About three months later, however, I received a cablegram from New York, asking me to come over right away. The new violist had broken down completely under the strain of travel and refused to continue any longer. Moreover, as he was more than ordinarily splenetic, some rather unpleasant episodes had occurred between him and his colleagues, and the overall situation pointed to eventual disaster. So I crossed the Atlantic in March 1930 and joined the quartet for the last third of the United States tour.

Joining the LSQ marked a demarcation line for me. I had become a violist full-fledged. I had burned all my bridges. Naturally I had quite a lot of work to do, as I had not played much of the literature from the violist's chair and the London Quartet's repertory was extensive. My colleagues, having finished a very strenuous season in the United States and having gone through a rather traumatic experience with their temporary violist, were not anxious to sit out long rehearsals for my benefit. We did rehearse, of course, on the voyage to South America, but the seductions of life on board, to say nothing of those on the boat deck, abetted by soft zephyrs and a tropical moon, supplanted the call of duty, and I was left pretty much to myself to sink or swim when we first appeared in Chile.

Warwick Evans

Fortunately our first concerts were in towns of minimal musical importance, so I was spared the ordeal of having to play before the critical and knowledgeable public that I was to encounter later in Santiago and elsewhere. I got through all right, despite a few mishaps such as wrong entries, which caused my hardened colleagues more amusement than animadversion. This was my first extensive foreign tour, my first exposure to exotic foods, and my inner workings, nurtured on plain, honest Scots fare—porridge, pease brose, haggis, and the like—rebelled and were reluctant to function.

Now I am by nature inclined to overdo remedial therapy. If a doctor prescribes three pills twice a day for a week, I will immediately take forty-two the first day for what I conceive to be a quicker cure! In this particular case beshrew me if I didn't imbibe a noble draft of a purgative abominated by all children. The result? During the concert, bowels of fierce fire and uproar! At a point in the music where I was supposed to change from alto to treble clef, so preoccupied was I with my distress I went straight ahead in the former, no doubt contributing to another kind of distress for the cognoscenti in the audience. This afforded my not-too-sympathetic colleagues a further source of wicked amusement and I was the butt of their ill-considered pleasantries for some time.

I found on this tour to South America that in the larger centers, such as Buenos Aires, Montevideo, São Paulo, and Santiago, the audiences were warm and sophisticated. In the smaller towns one never knew what to expect, which leads me to recount the remarkable and, in retrospect, hilarious occasion that was the foundation of the quartet's triumph in Latin America. Some years prior to my joining the LSQ, all future success of the quartet was assured by a concerted Bronx cheer from a section of the audience in Valparaiso, Chile. I don't wish to suggest that the quartet's great skill and dynamic personalities might not have prevailed without this evidence of displeasure, but it did not come amiss. Most of the concerts were given in movie theaters, as there were few conventional concert halls at that time except in the larger cities. In Valparaiso the theater was located at no great distance from the docks.

It was at the time that the movie of the Dempsey-Firpo fight was being shown throughout South America, and naturally Firpo was the hero, even though the loser. The quartet opened the matinee program with a Haydn opus and sensed a rather restless audience. Then proceeded a shorter and very effective work by Frank Bridge based on "Londonderry Air." It opens with three short, ejaculatory chords followed by a general pause. This happens three or four times before the actual working out of the folktune takes place. They played the first group of explosions, the general pause ensued, then the second group of explosions. By this time the "boys" in the gallery—mostly longshoremen who had come to see the fight film (actually scheduled for evening performance)—vigorously protested with the Chilean equivalent of a "raspberry." Warwick Evans signaled to his colleagues and the group forthwith exited. The local manager came to them in a frenzy of hot-blooded Latin distress, apologized profusely, vowed dire and terrible punishment on the sons of toil, and explained how the confusion arose.

The story got around to every important newspaper in South America: "This dishonor that has been visited upon Chilean appreciation of art and culture, this shocking insult to these distinguished visitors from Great Britain...." It *made* their tour.

We had other amusing experiences later on the tour when I was a member, such as the occasion when we arrived at a small town during an abominable rainstorm, suffering from mud, depression, and an utterly bad hotel. We were told that the manager of the theater had ordered the painting of a special backdrop for us. And what did we discover when we arrived at the theater? A completely nude and quite stout lady painted on this *mise en scène* for a string quartet concert, a Venus figure—but what a Venus! She would not have been out of place—save the execution of the drawing—in any Rubens, this obstreperous wench! We could scarce contain ourselves: this was the bawdiest daub we had ever seen.

Now, considering this an example of the local attitude toward art in general, we of course wondered what sort of an audience we were going to play to. We peered through the peephole in the fire curtain and could see only a small crowd at best—obviously not an audience that was going to listen to string quartet music with any great patience, although our Venus might assuage the general disappointment. So we cut the program considerably. In the Borodin D major quartet, for example, which we played at almost every concert, the Nocturne being an enormous favorite with all types of South American audiences, we cut out all expositions and developments and played the recapitulations and codas only. Our presentation was disposed of in about twelve minutes or less and the great unwashed paid us passing tribute with a sigh of relief.

Although most of my activities with the LSQ took place during the depression years, we somehow managed to keep on the tour until toward the end of that bitter period. Our 1932 tour, for example, was highlighted by the inauguration of Roosevelt, followed by the complete closing of all banks in the country a few days later. I happened to have cashed a check a day or two before and had about fifty dollars in my pocket. I was probably one of the wealthiest men in New York as far as actual currency went. At that time one met millionaires who didn't have a spendable penny. Then the problem of traveling arose, and we didn't know how we were going to pay our fares. The railroads accepted a scrip type of money that had been issued at the time, and we signed IOU's for the hotels. Everybody trusted everybody. Everybody had to, and the experience and the implications were certainly instructive and significant.

As we toured in those days, we also met with the embryonic idea of organized audiences. This embryo that was just becoming manifest eventually became the Civic Concerts and Community Concerts. Before that time artists might find themselves booked to play in Chicago, with the next stop in Seattle and after that St. Louis. A few artists, "box office specials," could insist on having their tours properly planned; but a quartet, even the Flonzaley or the London, didn't command the popular appeal that chamber music organizations do today and had to accept the crumbs as they fell from the table. Later in my career as a soloist I could travel to an important center such as Chicago, play a concert there, and stay in the area for a week, playing in Des Plaines, Highland Park, Evanston, and other residential districts around the city. They all had their own Community Concert series, which made it convenient and lucrative for an artist.

Some of the managerial selling techniques employed at the inception of the series are worth mentioning. This line, for example, was very typical: "You must hear the London String Quartet! You must see these gentlemen! Their clothes are tailored in London, shoes polished to such a height that you can see the reflection of your own face." And so on. This type of "selling" had nothing at all to do with the music; one could forget that.

But I must say we *were* different. If you look at contemporary pictures of the Flonzaley Quartet, which was as greatly renowned as the London Quartet, you see four very serious men with a considerable amount of whisker and longish hair and not the slightest hint of a smile. The picture of the LSQ, on the other hand, was usually enlivened with a little touch of vaudeville. In one shot that Warwick Evans thought up, only our heads appeared above his cello, which was laid on its side with the strings facing the camera. And there were other such poses that have become quite common in publicity pictures, such as four heads in line above each other. These pictures had a certain amount of theatricality because Evans felt— and quite rightly—that in places where we were trying to inculcate a new taste in very serious music the music should be introduced in a way that would not intimidate the public before it got to the concert. Once at a renowned public school in England Evans observed the notices that had been posted on the bulletin board, urging students to come to our *free* concert and warning them at the same time that chamber music is probably the most difficult of all forms of music to understand. Evans considered this poor promotion and said to the headmaster, "For heavens sake, how are you going to encourage a youngster to come to the concert if you post that warning?"

Warwick had a noteworthy, inventive capacity PR-wise and was ambitious and optimistic in his beliefs, as he demonstrated to the late critic, Olin Downes, who for some years ran a series of lecture recitals at the Brooklyn Academy. After engaging an artist, Downes went over the program beforehand in order to coordinate his lecture with the music to be performed. We were engaged for one of the series, and duly came Downes to our rehearsal. During the course of our discussions, Mr. Downes said he felt that perhaps the hall we were to perform in was too large for a string quartet. That raised Warwick Evans's hackles at once because he always maintained that if one string player could perform in Carnegie Hall, or some such auditorium, surely four could easily fill it with sound. When he protested and said he didn't think the Brooklyn Academy would be too large, the very serious Mr. Downes inquired, "Well, Mr. Evans, in your opinion what is the ideal hall for string quartet concerts?" In one of those great rejoinders which ring down through the ages, Warwick arose and declaimed, "Madison Square Garden at double prices!"

Originally the quartet must have presented a rather quaint appearance: Warwick Evans, very dark, with a chin like a battleship, was six feet three inches tall; John Pennington, the first violinist, with a profile as classic as John Barrymore's or Basil Rathbone's, was six feet four inches; Tommy Petre, the second violinist, was five feet six inches; and Waldo Warner, my predecessor, was even shorter. I am five feet eight inches tall, and I like to believe that when I replaced Warner I restored the symmetry to some degree.

John *was* a handsome man and, no mistake, a beautiful violinist to boot. Warwick presented a swashbuckling appearance, to say the least. He had very strong opinions about most things, sometimes

John Pennington

making himself considerably unpopular because of his fearless advocacy of his views. I must say, however, that I found myself in agreement with most of his musical opinions. Strictly speaking, Evans was not a learned musician, from the musicologist's point of view, but he was a very pragmatic one. Of the many things I heard later from Toscanini when I was with the NBC Symphony, there were very few that I had not learned first from Warwick Evans. He instinctively knew how things should go, how they should sound, how they should be presented to the listener—particularly Beethoven, whom he revered—and he persistently presented (and it took some persistence in those days) the full Beethoven quartet cycle. I

68

don't think the London String Quartet would have amounted to a thing if it hadn't been for Evans. So, as we have in our English history books Warwick the Kingmaker, I suggest that musical history will not hesitate to refer to Warwick the Quartetmaker.

In nearly all chamber groups one figure dominates, and in the LSQ it was Evans. Running a quartet on a democratic basis is completely unworkable, for usually one strong personality will dominate either by force of character or by methods of diplomacy. If he is diplomatic, he can achieve his end without too much friction. This is not necessarily always the first violinist. In fact, my experience of listening to many quartet groups *in the old days* convinced me that it was more often the cellist.

The reason may be readily conjectured. A quartet was made up of two violinists who usually fancied themselves a cut above the regular orchestra player but not quite good enough to present themselves as solo artists. The violist was usually, as we know to our sorrow, a disappointed violinist. The cellist was generally the best executant of the four because in those days he had no choice other than orchestra or quartet playing. The finer cellists reverted to the quartet—Hugo Becker, Piatti, Klengel, for example. There was a host of them. On the other hand, cellists as *solo* virtuosos emerged and had their day only after the advent of Casals and his successors, such as Piatigorsky, Fournier, Rostropovitch, and Starker, for example.

What I am trying to suggest is that in the quartet the cellists were in most cases considerably better players, more dominant musically and in every way than the two violinists and the violist. Of course there were always exceptions. As a rule, however, the cellist imposed his ideas and will upon the others. And Warwick Evans, as cellist, dominated the LSQ from the beginning. It was his idea to form a quartet in the first place in 1908, and the successful career of the quartet was the result of his planning and force of character.

I include the business side as well. After World War I the quartet toured Spain, and out of that came their invitation to play in South America. I recollect Evans telling me he had to use forceful tactics, including the vigorous twisting of a British cabinet minister's arm, in order to make the tour to Spain possible. I honestly believe the LSQ would not have succeeded if it hadn't been for Warwick Evans.

Finally by 1935 the depression had such an effect on the economy of the country that touring with a string quartet became a losing proposition. We decided, therefore, that instead of lingering on in

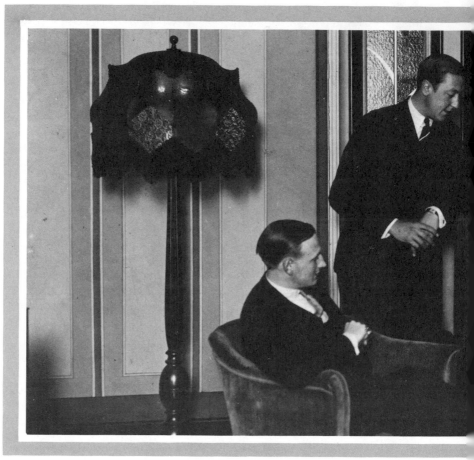

The LSQ in the 1930s. Primrose is seated

an agonizing financial death we should disband while we were still on top and go our own ways. In time I joined the NBC Symphony and the other three gravitated to the studios in Hollywood.

Considerably later Mrs. E. S. Coolidge, that noble patroness of chamber music and a very close friend of Warwick, suggested to him that the quartet might be brought together during the summer to perform at the various festivals she never tired of organizing. After a successful and joyous reconvening in 1939 and subsequent summers, Evans was once again assailed by the virus—which was not unexpected—and wished the quartet to function as of old on a full-time annual basis. But my orchestra and later solo assignments

made this impossible for me. Another viola player was recruited and the quartet continued spasmodically into the 1950s, when, like the old soldier in celebrated song, it simply faded away.

Although quartet playing is usually serious business, some occasions were rather amusing and bring delight when I reflect on them. We each had a good sense of the ludicrous and relished incidents that might well have raised not a modicum of hilarity in another group.

As for the London Quartet, I remember in particular one concert during the Beethoven cycle, which we were offering at Harvard University. It was inevitable that we would come to the time when the *Grosse Fuge* would have to be performed in its proper station, in a beautiful, old, but rather drafty theater. I was sitting beside Pennington, according to the seating arrangement in the LSQ, when suddenly I noticed that his page was beginning to flap about in the breeze. I began to feel more than a little apprehensive, for, as is well known, if you get out in the *Grosse Fuge* its complexity is such that you might as well start all over again. I reached over to push the page down with my bow, but when I returned to play my own part I had lost my place. It could have been catastrophic if I had also lost my head. There are various sections to the fugue and I knew that I would find my place eventually, though at the moment I was hopelessly at sea. So I went through the motions of playing with the bow about a sixteenth of an inch off the string (which difficult technique I invite anyone to try sometime) until we came to the following section, a few bars later.

I don't wish to give the impression that I was always the cause of humor in the quartet. On the other hand, I do seem to have been the subject of a fair share of incidents—for example, one that occurred during the first full season I played with the LSQ. The New York concerts drew nigh, and the other members were becoming quite nervous in my behalf. Not that they thought I would let them down, but here was I, a new viola player, and they had talked rather extravagantly about me, I am inclined to think. I was not unduly apprehensive, for by that time I was completely at home in the work I was doing and knew our repertoire very well—almost by heart.

We were engaged to play a concert at Town Hall. On the program were the Brahms B-flat quartet, which features the viola in no little degree, and the Debussy quartet, which doesn't stint the viola either. After arriving early at Town Hall, I decided to go out and stroll in the pleasant, salubrious spring evening. I lit a cigarette, stupidly forgot to close the match cover, and the whole thing flared up in my hand. I sustained a severe burn on my left hand and was tolerably perturbed and concerned.

Wherefor I hied me to a drugstore and asked for something to allay the pain. The druggist gave me a medication that lessened the pain somewhat, but unfortunately it was also a very sticky substance. One of the areas that was badly burned was the ball of my left thumb, to which I applied the medication generously. So there I was during the concert, shifting around with my thumb coming unstuck and getting restuck, certain that everyone in the audience must have heard the noise, even the critics in the back row. There was also an agonizing burn between my first and second fingers, and every time I played a half step I really suffered from the ensuing friction. I got through the concert, nevertheless, and even through the reception later in the evening. And I received compliments and congratulations on my performance of the important viola sections.

Later, on our way back to the hotel, Warwick took me aside and said, "Look, don't you know better than to talk to people with your hand in your pocket, especially to ladies? You've had your left hand stuck in your pocket all evening."

"Yes, I do know," I said, "but *you* know how badly I burned my hand?"

His immediate response was to suppose that my hand was too sore to expose, but I explained to him that it was not so much that as the fact that if people had seen my burned hand, instead of complimenting me they would have said something like, "Yes, Primrose played quite well. But it's a shame! If only he hadn't hurt his hand...." I didn't bemoan my predicament and I didn't let anybody observe the injury.

I have maintained that attitude throughout all my professional life. Never complain and never make explanations, because the immediate reaction on the part of the listener will always be, "Yes, he did well enough, but..." I think Warwick appreciated the point. These things I look upon as part of being a professional. I think there are certain things that a professional does and those that an amateur does, and they should never be confused.

The LSQ was one of the most prominent chamber ensembles of the day, but unfortunately we made very few recordings. When Albert Sammons was the first violinist, he had solo ambitions, as I previously related—and understandably so. The quartet was not so busy in its early days before World War I that Albert couldn't take time off to pursue his ambition. For one thing, he made a contract with a recording outfit in England known as the Aeolian-Vocalian Company. English Columbia approached the LSQ at the same time to make recordings, but Sammons wouldn't agree to this, for he wished to remain loyal to Aeolian-Vocalian. As a *douceur*, A-V made several quite unimportant recordings of the quartet. Columbia, in the meantime, engaged the Lener Quartet, made countless recordings, built them up, promoted them, and spent a good deal of money in the process, all of which would have benefited the LSQ if Sammons hadn't felt this allegiance.

A similar luckless turn of events befell me later on. After I left the London Quartet, my next professional quartet experience of importance came with the Primrose Quartet. This group was organized during the late thirties and early forties when I was a member of the NBC Symphony. I had done a great deal of recording for RCA as a soloist, and the Primrose Quartet had made a few records for the same company. Moses Smith of Columbia Records heard us play, liked what he heard, and asked if we would record the complete Beethoven quartets for Columbia, which would have constituted an outstanding opportunity. I had played Beethoven quartets with the London group until they were coming out of my fingers and had very strong opinions as to how they should be performed. And I don't hesitate to say frankly that I very rarely hear what to me is a satisfactory performance of a Beethoven quartet.

I went to my old friend, the late Charles O'Connell, who was the counterpart of Smith at RCA, and told him, "Charles, we've had an offer from Columbia. I don't want to accept it if you'd rather we stick with RCA. I think the quartet would like to do this if you feel you can assure us of a good recording future." He asked that we please not forswear our allegiance, continuing that he was sure we could make all the recordings we wished for his company. So we turned down Moses Smith—and who got the job? The Budapest Quartet! The snows of yesteryear fell once again. They recorded the entire Beethoven cycle and we all know what a career emerged from that! As it turned out, there are very few recordings available now of the Primrose Quartet. In fact, it was difficult for us to perform very much in public because we could seldom get away from our orchestral duties, and one has to perform publicly to stimulate record sales.

The Primrose Quartet came into being at the solicitation of the NBC music department in 1938. Actually two quartets were recruited from the redoubtable ranks of Toscanini's strings: the Primrose Quartet and the NBC Quartet. Any successful administration always has two of the same thing so that one can be played off against the other! Incidentally, the choice of the name "Primrose Quartet" was made by NBC, not by me. I suppose there might have been a few previous occasions when a quartet adopted the name of the violist, but it was most unusual. I was embarrassed, thinking this was a considerable reflection on my colleagues, but they behaved in an irreproachable fashion and the title was never a source of friction.

Naturally, the music department did not have to press their solicitation, as I was ardent in my desire to return to my first and great-

PHOTO PRINTED BY PERMISSION FROM AMERICAN STRING TEACHER, SUMMER 1968, P. 36

The Primrose Quartert in 1940. Left to right: Oskar Shumsky, Josef Gingold, Harvey Shapiro, and Primrose

est love in music—quartet playing. Josef Gingold, an Ysaÿe alumnus, was also an avid chamber music buff. We happened to strike a very friendly and musically profitable association with Harvey Shapiro, a cellist in the NBC Symphony. Mr. Gingold didn't particularly wish to take on the first violin position, so we searched for a player to fill the vacancy until we happened to hear a youth, Oscar Shumsky, who impressed us with his overwhelming talent.

I have already commented on what was formerly the usual composition of string quartets, namely the slightly indifferent virtuosi as violinists, the violist from the violin scrap heap, and finally the cellist, who was as a rule the best player and musician of the bunch. However, I am quite convinced—and I am conceited enough to say so—that no quartet ever played that had the instrumental ability of my quartet. Oscar Shumsky is one of the greatest virtuosos I have ever heard. That he didn't make an international career as a soloist

PHOTO BY CHARLES PETERSON

The Primrose Quartet warming up for a game of cricket

is one of those mysteries that crop up in the profession all the time.* Then, of course, there were Jo Gingold's abilities as a violinist, and Harvey Shapiro was a superior cellist indeed. The group had no cripple; we all played in a virtuoso manner.

I have always admonished students never to play quartets in the manner so frequently encountered. The procedure is *not* to sit

---

*That Shumsky has since attained to Olympian heights as a violinist, violist (in his less responsible moments), and conductor, admired by all his colleagues, is consolation to those of us who deplored his earlier obscurity.

down on the chair and be modest. If they undertake to play a Beethoven quartet, they must realize, first of all, that—in the late quartets especially—the first violin part, from a technical and musical standpoint, is in many cases considerably more demanding than the violin concerto. Why should it be played in a diffident manner? One can observe the numerous occasions in the Haydn quartets, particularly in the slow movements, where the first violinist takes off on a tremendous coloratura unfoldment. In these very elaborate passages, when the violinist should go winging into the empyrean, too often I heard him play with an utter lack of imagination and an abundance of modesty—no *panache*; no conceit.

As to the violist, I have sometimes heard that this is a downright thankless job. I must say that if it is a thankless job it is very often the fault of a thankless player who plays in a thankless manner, making thankless music. Playing the viola gave me much more pleasure than I ever had playing the violin.

The viola is the liaison between the cello and the violins. A series of reiterated notes, for example, which appears on paper to be only a somewhat dull accompaniment, must be played in a manner that allows it almost to burst into song itself in the player's effort to sustain and nourish the lofty theme to which it is the handmaiden. The violist can readily influence the person who has the thematic material to play better if he "plays" the other part in his part. I am disposed to believe that, with all due modesty, a prime example is the slow movement of the Mozart B-flat duo in my recording with Heifetz.

This attitude and approach should be adopted by the violist as a kind of credo. So often the viola carries the important contrapuntal material. Note Mozart's writing, for example, with its mastery of *living* counterpoint, as opposed to Proutian or the "it-looks-good-on-paper" kind. One voice can actually be dropped from most Mozart quartets and result in very satisfying string trios. In Mozart's G minor quintet the first violin may absent himself for the first two bars of the third movement, the resulting quartet still being the envy of many another composer, with an entirely different melody dominating in the first viola part.

The great contrapuntalists wrote in such a way that no part is unimportant. They conceived nothing as mere accompaniment, just as there's no such thing, in my judgment, as a "second" violin. I always talk to my students about the *other* violin, *not* the second violin. Using the word *second* too often prompts a subordinate approach in the student's mind and he tends to play like a second violin. There is the charming account of the lady who, at the end of a quartet concert, approached one of the musicians and asked if she might look at his instrument, saying, "I've never seen a second violin before." A successful quartet will always emerge from a situation in which the "second" violin is trying to outplay the "first." I don't mean that there should be vulgar or obtrusive competition, but the second violinist should perform in a manner that may prompt the listener to reflect, "I wonder why Mr. B is playing the second part. Surely he is just as good as Mr. A, who's playing first." When Mr. B is obviously a "second" violinist, however, the quartet fails to that degree.

Of course, there is also the opposite situation. In one classic story a knowledgeable aficionado was asked, "Can you tell us exactly what is a string quartet?" He answered, "Yes, it's usually composed of four men, each of whom thinks he is saving the situation."

I've enjoyed every quartet I've played. My annual revel with the London group was the performance of the Beethoven cycle. Of the three Brahms, the Opus 67 brought particular pleasure, not necessarily because the viola predominates in one of the movements, but because of the consistent strength of the entire work. Of the two highly regarded French works, I experience infinitely greater satisfaction playing the Ravel quartet than the Debussy. I have always approached the Fauré G minor piano quartet with great eagerness. I know of no work that evokes in me the essence, the soul and spirit, of Paris more than this one does. What an urbane and highly civilized composer he was!

My deep regret is that I never played a Bartók quartet. That may sound incredible because of my later affiliation with Bartók and his viola concerto and the immense attention paid to them now. But when I was a member of the LSQ in the early thirties, hardly anybody played Bartók. It was considered an enormity to play his works, and quartets were almost run out of town for attempting to do so. As far as I am aware, only the Kolisch Quartet dared such a venture in those days. When I had my own quartet at NBC in the late thirties and early forties, the situation was almost the same. Later, when I came to coach Bartók quartets in class, I was filled with regret, for they are great chamber works—moving pieces, replete with beauty, originality, and invention.

Poor Bartók. Forty years ago when he essayed to play his own music, he was scorned by the majority of listeners. Though he had his admirers and people who were faithful to him, such as Szigeti, they were few and far between. It is only since he cleverly managed to die destitute that he has become popular. I suspect that the American public, as usual, overreacted to a plethora of guilt feelings.

The late Quincy Porter once asked me why I didn't play more often the concerto he wrote for me. I think it is a fine work and rewardingly written for the violist, as Porter played viola himself. I told him, "Quincy, unless you can become notorious in some way, run off with an infamous and wealthy heiress or jump off a building, it will be difficult to get your concerto performed."

My ability to give in to any temptation to play quartets led me into an interesting association with Kreisler, which was for the sole purpose of recording his own quartet. Other collaboration with him was very much of the "let's sit down and have fun" variety. I had met Kreisler years before at the home of Dr. Frederic Bierhof in New York. The latter was an eminent physician, very fond of music, whose opulent apartment was a mecca for musicians. There I played chamber music informally with Kreisler, and it was an ingratiating experience.

On one occasion, before I had the means to travel en luxe, I found myself sailing across the Atlantic aboard the same ship with Kreisler. That I was traveling second class and he first is a glimpse of the obvious, to be sure, but when he heard that I was on board he invited me to dine with him; and after that we spent quite a lot of time in the first class section together, to my continuing comfort. He knew my reputation from the LSQ and later asked me, along with my colleague Tom Petre, to join him in recording his own A minor quartet for HMV in London. He also invited Lauri Kennedy, the superb Australian cellist and then the principal cellist of the BBC Orchestra. Lauri had toured Great Britain and the United States as "comic relief" with the tenor John McCormack, just as I did years later with Richard Crooks, only Lauri had a much less pleasant experience.

Kreisler obviously inherited his inspiration from Schubert—the whole spirit, everything. Those were the 78 rpm days, when we had to play correctly for approximately four and one-half minutes, and it was always something of a strain. We spent two days recording the quartet, and it soon became evident that we were going to have a blank side—something the recording companies didn't care for. It was suggested that Kreisler write a piece for the odd side, or, better still, that he might score one of his violin transcriptions for quartet, which he did. I sat in his hotel room while he made the arrangement right then and there of something that was attributed to Boc-

Recording the Kreisler A minor quartet in London at the famous Abbey Road Studio. Left to right: Fritz Kreisler, Primrose, Lauri Kennedy, and Thomas Petre

cherini, whereupon I rushed the score to the copyist. We recorded it the next day, and when we were through Kreisler thanked the three of us for having allowed the "amateur" to play with us.

I saw him finally one summer evening in the mid-fifties at Tanglewood when I was playing *Harold in Italy* again—the inevitable and ubiquitous *Harold*—with Munch. Kreisler was in the audience, and he came backstage at the close of the concert. A large number of people were in the artist's room, milling around, talking to me

and to Munch. Then Kreisler entered, and suddenly there was a profound hush. He thanked Munch, thanked me, congratulated us, and left. By that time Fritz was very deaf and hadn't played in quite a long time. I hope that someday the Kreisler Quartet in A Minor will be reissued. It is indeed significant and instructive to listen to Kreisler playing a string quartet.*

*The recording has recently been released and may be obtained from Education Media, P.O. Box 921, Berkeley, California.

Primrose and Fritz Kreisler

My subsequent affiliation with another group, the Heifetz-Primrose-Piatigorsky Trio, grew out of Heifetz's and my recording of duos in the late thirties and our later association with Emanuel Feuermann. Fortunately we were able to record the Mozart Divertimento in E-flat and the Dohnányi Serenade with Feuermann before he died. His loss was shattering.

The story goes that Feuermann underwent a relatively minor operation that was badly performed and that was that. He didn't survive. I could hardly credit this, because I had seen him in New York only a week or two before, and my parting had been, "Mounyo, I'll see you in California in about three weeks and we'll get started on those Beethoven trios with Jascha." I arrived in Hollywood, checked into my hotel, and called Heifetz to ask when we would start rehearsing and he exclaimed, "Haven't you heard? Don't you know about the Feuermann tragedy?" I thought immediately that perhaps his mother-in-law or even his wife had died. I certainly never associated Emanuel with the impersonality of death. He was so full of life and vigor, and so vivid. When Heifetz conveyed the news, I was shocked and bewildered.

I thought at the time that Heifetz would probably call on Piatigorsky to take the place of Feuermann, but this was a case parallel to the unexpected death of Nikolai Graudan of the Festival Quartet years later: our group had been a personal association that was disrupted by death, and similarly Heifetz made up his mind that he wasn't going to continue the recordings with another cellist. But unlike a few other things that Heifetz determined on one particular day, and determined in an adamant way, his decision gradually altered over the years and eventually Piatigorsky was called to service.

Despite Feuermann's greatness, I fear that the memory of him has faded. This is not totally unexpected, however. Many young students today, when asked who Kreisler is or was, or if they have heard of Ysaÿe, often reply with only a blank stare. Once an artist ceases to record or perform, his reputation gradually evanesces. I think of Kreisler, for instance. He never taught, so he left nothing behind in that respect. He wrote no major musical work, though his transcriptions and short pieces are unique. But they are very seldom heard today in recital programs. His most enduring legacy is his cadenzas for the standard concertos, particularly the Beethoven and the Brahms. It is not easy to get a Kreisler recording today; hence he really left little to posterity.*

Feuermann was a lesser figure, certainly not because of his playing, but because he appeared so briefly on the musical scene in this country before his death. When he did play, the impact was prodigious. He had a stupendous technique and a bow of infinite facility. The end of the fourth movement of the Dohnányi Serenade, where he has but a few simple phrases to play, is almost unbearably heartrending.

I spoke earlier of the Fauré G minor piano quartet. The piano quartet combination of instruments is perhaps uncommon but leaves a definite impact. I appeared in 1947 at the Edinburgh Festival with Schnabel, Szigeti, and Fournier in such presentation. We had glorious, relaxed, and occasionally amusing times together, and thereby hangs a cricket story. We started our rehearsals in the latter part of August, and the weather was unusually magnanimous for

---

*Since this writing a number of vintage Kreisler recordings have become available, *particularly* the Beethoven and the Brahms concertos, which I discovered to my unbounded joy in the Yamaha emporium in the Ginza (Tokyo) not long ago.

London. The twenty-third of August was a Saturday and my birthday. I was very anxious to go that afternoon to Lord's Cricket Ground, where I have been a member of the club since 1935. The situation of the match was such that I dearly wanted to be there; but when we finished our rehearsal around midday, Schnabel announced, "We will have lunch and then meet at two o'clock."

I was aghast, but suddenly had an inspiration. "Mr. Schnabel," I said, "this is my birthday." He congratulated me congenially, and I added, "You know, there are quite a few people I would like to see this afternoon."

"Certainly," he said, "we'll continue to rehearse tomorrow."

I didn't tell him there were about thirty thousand people I wanted to see. I got away with it but divulged my double-crossing to him years later. In the interim Schnabel had become very friendly with Neville Cardus, later Sir Neville, our foremost cricket authority, as well as a music critic of no mean repute, who interested Schnabel in the game. When I subsequently told Schnabel the true story, he said, "I wouldn't have understood then, but if it happened now I might go with you."

I had profound admiration for Schnabel—and great affection. He was a difficult man to many, not everybody's cup of tea, but I liked him immensely and we got on well together. For example, there was the famous occasion of our last concert at the first Edinburgh Festival in 1947. At this final concert in packed Usher Hall, to an audience at once expectant and regretful—regretful that the series had come to its end—we opened with the C minor Brahms quartet. Schnabel played his introductory octave C (or, more precisely, double octave C), and we hadn't proceeded as far as the end of the first string phrase when my C-string broke. In those days I used to carry two instruments, so I merely left the platform and the huge audience, got the other viola, came back and started again. About halfway through the first page Szigeti's E-string, not to be outdone, gave way. (I might add that it's no secret Szigeti had a great battle with his nerves all his playing career, which is why I feel that his was a heroic one. I could never have endured what he so consistently suffered.) Joshka carried his strings in his pocket, but by this time events had so unnerved him that he had ample trouble putting the string in the peg box. When all was set once more, I turned to Schnabel and said, "All right, it's your turn now," which he thought so funny he could scarce contain himself.*

*A recent contributor to a certain "Letters to the Editor" column offers a considerably different version of this incident. Mine is the authentic one. After all, I was there!

He was a man who never assaulted the piano. I never once heard hammer hit string, and yet he could achieve an eloquent abundance of sound. It was almost as if he gently and firmly squeezed out the tone as you would squeeze the juice out of an orange. It was, in fine, an experience high above common expectation for me to have played with him. His English was impeccable and his vocabulary extensive. The books he wrote and lectures he gave were cultured and erudite. He was always on the lookout for a fight, especially with a critic. It's not that he was ill-tempered or overly combative, but he had very high ideals and was completely uncompromising. This made him difficult for many people, but not for me. All of his students adored him, and so did sundry others.

I will never forget his performance of the G major concerto by Beethoven at the same festival. I was backstage when he came in, barely a few minutes before he had to appear on stage. He divested himself of his overcoat, proceeded in leisurely manner to the platform, and gave a performance that I will preserve in my memory forever. I can never forget the little scale in the first phrase—the beauty and the eloquence of every note. But that was his way. He bewitched and enchanted his listener.

The Festival Piano Quartet was perhaps the most unexpected chamber group with which I performed. It so happened that Victor Babin, the pianist; Szymon Goldberg, the violinist; Nicolai Graudan, the cellist; and myself were more or less thrown together at the Aspen Institute in the summer of '53. We played one program of piano quartets there on command, and suddenly I was struck with the idea that it would be a rewarding thing to surrender a few weeks each year of our personal concert tours, make perhaps a dozen appearances together, and have an amiable cooperation. The idea developed rather rapidly and, to our astonishment, by the time our first season got underway we found we were engaged to play thirty concerts in as many days. And we made recordings to boot.

At the close of our fifth season Graudan went to Russia to visit relatives (he hadn't been there since the Revolution), and in the course of his congé collapsed of a fatal aneurysm. Because it had been such a very personal thing—four friends making music together—we didn't relish bringing in another cellist, and so we disbanded.

At this point I can't refrain from telling how I surreptitiously got my colleagues into a plane piloted by myself. But first I should provide the background to my aspirations as a pilot. Just after the war ended, when it was impossible to get accommodations on any transatlantic ship, I made one round-trip flight to Europe. The ex-

Festival Quartet. Left to right: Szymon Goldberg, Victor Babin, Nicolai Graudan, and Primrose

perience was not encouraging, since at that time planes were falling out of the skies right and left, with the expected fatal results. I developed a rooted aversion to flying, as did a number of my colleagues, Milstein and Menuhin, to name but two. My reluctance to fly was vastly inconvenient and no doubt cost me concert appearances.

Some years later, in 1956, I was in London discussing my European tour for the approaching season with my English manager, Mrs. Tillet, when she informed me that my first appearance would be with the BBC Orchestra in London and two days later I was invited to appear in Helsinki. That meant flying, of course. Would I do it? I had played in Helsinki before and enjoyed the experience so much that after a moment's hesitation I said with pathetic bravado, "All right, into the bright blue yonder!" When I left her office I thought to myself: Miserable fool! Now you're faced with six months at least of sleepless nights worrying about the flight.

I was persuaded there was only one way to kill my dread. I hailed a taxi and asked to be driven to the London Airport. When the jehu asked, "Which line?" I was confounded for a moment until

I remembered seeing advertisements for British-European Airlines, and I knowingly asked for BEA. I just managed to coincide with the deluxe champagne lunch flight to Paris. I had never before been in a plane such as a Viscount, so vast it seemed with its large windows, sleek lines, and *Möet et Chandon* stimulation. It was prop-driven, a form of propulsion I had never experienced before. The view was captivating, the flight pleasant, the lunch *cordon bleu,* and the landing smooth at Le Bourget. I didn't go into Paris; I boarded the return flight immediately and returned to London.

That cured the neurosis and replaced it with an immediate passion for flying. I determined to learn to fly myself. I did. I enjoyed it immensely. I have never regretted it. I even did a lot of cross-country flying, usually for professional reasons while touring, but I always had a qualified pilot in the right-hand seat because I didn't care to take the sole responsibility on such short experience.

The Festival Quartet flew to all destinations. Sometimes, if we were obliged to wait for an hour or so for a connection, I rented a plane and flew to the destination myself. But I could never get my colleagues to fly with me, either singly or collectively. They simply would not hazard it, and I suppose I can understand their reluctance.

The rules in the United States very strictly prohibit anyone's entering the cockpit—except hijackers, apparently. But in Canada, where my colleagues and I were touring at this particular remove, the rules were slightly more relaxed. Thus it was not irregular when the young French-Canadian pilot, upon noticing the AOPA badge on my lapel—that's Aircraft Owners and Pilots Association—invited me into the cockpit. I had been there only a few minutes when he vacated his seat and offered me the controls. Once a plane is in the air, it is no great task to keep it going. You've got to be a bit of an idiot to crash it. So I flew for about a half-hour, keeping the aircraft straight and level, altering the compass headings as instructed.

I then returned to the cabin and confronted my friends. Graudan was asleep, Szymon was immersed in a score, as he invariably was, and Victor was reading a book. "How are you enjoying the flight?" I ventured. Everyone agreed it was "marvelous," "beautiful," "a wonderful flight!"

"Capital," I said, "I've been flying the plane!" There was a minor riot. They were going to write the government, they were going to sue somebody—I don't recall what else they were going to do—they were so incensed. But I reminded them, "We're still aloft, you know."

Toscanini

7

Conductors

I have already mentioned that I was affiliated with the NBC Symphony for a while. After the dissolution of the London String Quartet in 1935, and before I became a member of NBC, I did almost everything and anything that came to hand because my financial cable was broken and the anchor lost. The night before I gave my first performance of the Walton concerto with Beecham and the Royal Philharmonic Society, I was in a theater pit playing entr'acte music. When the actors were busy onstage, I practiced the Walton. I don't think any of this hurt. Actually I think this sort of experience is very good, as was the experience I had with Sir Thomas at the performance, learning how to keep my head and to refrain from indulging in hysterics.

Rehearsals for the concerto were adequate, but Beecham attended only the final one. His concertmaster, himself a very good conductor, undertook the initial rehearsals. One may imagine my feelings: the great occasion, the Royal Philharmonic Society, my first appearance there, my first performance of the Walton, a packed house and distinguished audience—and Sir Thomas Beecham became completely and utterly lost during the Scherzo. When that sort of thing happened, and it did from time to time, Beecham went into what I called his "fencing act." In other words, he used his baton as one might use an *épée*. The terpsichorean antics he went through, of course, had nothing at all to do with the music being played.

Fortunately the orchestra knew the work very well. The concertmaster beat time, wielding the scroll of his fiddle, and we survived. Beecham—bless his heart—turned to me afterward and, with that bland, exophthalmic effrontery so uniquely his, he said in a not inaudible aside, "Well, at least we finished together, dear boy!" It was difficult to subdue a feeling of triumph. A stunning moment. One night I was playing in a theater pit and the next night I was playing to a distinguished audience in Queens Hall, with a great orchestra and an eminent conductor, and near disaster.

During this period I played on the Continent quite often, particularly in Italy—a country and an audience I came to love. Fees were not particularly high, nor was there much profit left over after a continental tour, what with all the expenses of traveling and the temptation to spend money in foreign countries. Italian audiences weren't especially well-behaved either, as I later found German audiences to be. The Italians were inclined to chatter, and a good deal of shuffling went on during a concert. The audiences were very volatile, very lively. At first I found this rather disconcerting, but I soon grew used to it.

On several occasions I performed at La Scala, where the acoustics graveled me. As a member of the audience listening to opera, I could hardly have wished for more perfect acoustical properties. On stage, however, things sounded quite otherwise. It was like playing up against a blanket. Fortunately I had become used to that sort of trial and knew that the last thing one should do was to force the sound, to try to force it through the blanket. But it is always disquieting to feel that the apparently smoke-dry sonance is not traveling much more than an inch beyond the F-holes of the instrument.

A delightful feature of playing in Italy was that country's custom of paying in cash at the end of a concert. Japanese custom evokes a similar euphoria for the same reason. After the war I was paid a not inadequate fee, even by American standards. The exchange was then thousands of *lire* to the dollar, and I was acquiring a prodigious amount of those large, attractive notes. Replete with beauty, those bills would have made such handsome wallpaper. I hated to exchange them for dollars. I stuffed them into my pockets and into my viola case and my accompanist filled the briefcase with the intemperate superfluity. We didn't give even one fleeting thought to walking back to the hotel. Of course if we had done that in New York we'd have been dead before we'd gone half a block.

I made only one appearance in Germany before the war, and that was in Berlin during the Hitler era. On this occasion the Berlin Philharmonic gave an all-English concert. I essayed the Vaughan Williams suite, and the Walton symphony plus a Bax overture filled the remainder of the bill. The Germans wined and dined Walton and myself in princely vogue, and we had the run of the beautiful premises known as the *Deutsch Englische Gesellschaft*. We were heavily propagandized. A very cultured gentlemen tried to clarify what was happening in Germany by explaining that though we British had a venerable history that issued from our native soil centuries ago the Germans had a new country and no history and therefore had to expand. Rather specious reasoning I concluded at the time. He was not referring to *Lebensraum*, but to the Germans' need to expand culturally and to the fact that Germany's natural friend, Great Britain, is almost a member of the family, sharing the same roots culturally and racially.

Hitler was not in attendance at the concert, but some of the Nazi hierarchy were there. And some Jews were still in the Berlin Philharmonic, which was interesting to observe. Furtwängler did protect them, including the personnel manager, but it wasn't long before he and the other Jews had to hotfoot it out of Hitler's realm.

At the Berlin concert an assistant to Furtwängler, Leo Borchard, conducted. Probably his only, and unfortunate, claim to fame rests in the fact that after the war when he was to conduct the RIAS Orchestra in the western sector of Berlin he passed a checkpoint one day without identifying himself and was shot to death by a sentry.

Later at the Lucerne Festival in 1950 I played with Furtwängler, whom I found very aloof. I was due to perform the *Schwanendreher* by Hindemith, and I felt Furtwängler didn't have much sympathy with that kind of music. He took no trouble to prepare it, and when he came to the 7/8 bar in the last movement he was completely at sea. I'm sure that with a couple of minutes' effort he would have been able to direct it, but he didn't trouble himself. He just wobbled his notoriously wobbly arms and relied on the experienced orchestra to remedy the situation.

It was in Italy that I first met Toscanini. At the time the LSQ officially disbanded, Toscanini was still directing the New York Philharmonic. Alfred Wallenstein, who was then the first cellist, told me he was certain the solo viola position in the orchestra would shortly be up for grabs. Knowing that I was returning to Europe, he suggested that I make a point of going to Milano, getting in touch with the maestro, and playing for him. Thus I went to Milano, stayed in a rather charming but cheap *albergo,* and found my way to Toscanini's apartment in the Via Durini. I had written him in advance, telling him that I was coming and that Mr. Wallenstein had suggested I play for him. I thought this would elicit an immediate response, since he and Wallenstein were very close. When I heard nothing at all, which rather raised my hackles, I determined to force myself on him.

I was and have always been somewhat retiring and unpresumptuous, too proud to importune; but having traveled so far and at such expense (that is, such expense for my resources as they were then), I summoned my courage to do what otherwise would have presented itself as outrageous and impossible. I went with my viola to his apartment, which occupied the whole of the second floor. Looking across the courtyard, I could see Toscanini lunching with a few guests. When the maid answered the door, I took a stab at Spanish, having no Italian at the time, and asked whether Maestro Toscanini was at home. Of course she said no. I then took her by the arm, led her into the corridor, pointed across the courtyard, and demanded, "Isn't that Maestro Toscanini eating lunch?"

"Yes," she said.

"Well," I said, "I would like to see him. You tell him Mr. Primrose is here."

She went off, leaving me standing outside the hallway, and the next thing I knew, Toscanini opened the door and invited me in. I sat in his music room while he finished lunch. When he came back, we discussed the possibility of my playing in his orchestra. I played for him, and he seemed well enough pleased. That was the end of the interview. I heard nothing more. Shortly after that, Toscanini resigned his leadership of the New York Philharmonic.

Some time later I read an article about the pending formation of the NBC Symphony. It was at the time Samuel Chotzinoff went to Italy to try to persuade Toscanini to come back. By the way, I had a sneaking suspicion that it wasn't nearly so difficult to persuade him as we were led to believe. I think a man would have to be made of much sterner stuff than any of us are made of to be able to resist an offer of so many thousands of dollars per concert, free of income tax, with a hand-picked orchestra and a riverside mansion to live in.

It was suggested that I get in touch with NBC and audition for a position in the orchestra. Believe it or not, for some reason I'll never understand, I was reluctant to do so. I had by now reverted to my rather retiring disposition. These events all took place about the time my recording of the two Paganini caprices reached the United States. A friend of mine in New York took the recording to Samuel Chotzinoff, who heard it together with the personnel manager, Leo Spitalny. They immediately invited me to come for an interview. I was interested for several reasons. Up to that point I had never played in a symphony orchestra and felt that this was a facet of my musical development that was regrettably lacking. Also, I was determined to find out whether Toscanini was really the ogre described by so many musicians.

At this point I would like to clear up a general misapprehension regarding this matter of my position in the viola section. I have always been regarded as the first violist of the NBC Symphony and publicity has always stressed the fact. But this is not true. If my recording of the caprices had come to the attention of the NBC authorities a week or so earlier, I might have been the first violist without challenge. As it was, Artur Rodzinski, who was charged with organizing and preparing the orchestra for the maestro, doing the donkey work, as it were, had enlisted his own first violist from Cleveland, Carlton Cooley. It was never clearly understood that at the most this was a joint tenure. As Cooley was engaged before I was, Rodzinski certainly wasn't going to demote him. I have found from firsthand experience, however, that it is quite difficult to refute a story once it gets into public domain. I was inexperienced as an orchestra player and had to depend a great deal on Cooley at first. I think I caught on fairly quickly, though.

Poor Rodzinski, despite his best efforts, brought the wrath of the maestro down upon himself on one occasion at least. Toscanini arrived in the United States several days before he was due to assume command. Once in a while we observed him standing outside in the corridor listening to the rehearsal. Rodzinski nearly always rehearsed sitting on a high stool with his very long legs wrapped around each other. One day he was talking with Toscanini and apologizing for the lack of spirit in the orchestra at a particular rehearsal. The maestro immediately berated him, saying, "How you expect orchestra to play when you sit down? If you lazy, then they lazy!"

Toscanini's first experience with us, and ours with him, was the Brahms C minor symphony. We went through it without interruption until the brass chorale in the introduction to the last movement. It didn't suit him and he stopped: "Signori, you play like that, you not my friends!" I thought the furies were about to sling their flames, but we were spared these till later.

I soon found out, of course, that the reports of Toscanini's violent temper were well founded. Sitting as close to him as I did for four years, I began to notice quite a number of things. I noticed, for instance, that if he came to rehearsal with a sallow complexion we were in for a bad time. But if, on the contrary, he had a slight flush on his cheeks—he had beautiful skin, almost like a child's—then I knew we were about to be gentled with comely address. Obviously he was a liverish man; and when his liver was affected and he became sallow, the storm raged. As Goldsmith would have it:

> Well had the boding tremblers learned to trace
> The day's disasters in his morning face.

I realized on one occasion that some of those outbursts were calculated. We were working on one of the lesser-known works by Respighi. The score that Toscanini had on his stand was, I was told, the only one in America. We were at war at the time and did not have access to music published in Italy. Losing his temper at one point, and raging, stamping, and bellowing, he picked up the score and was about to hurl it to the floor, but he stopped with it in midair, his hands uplifted. You could almost follow his thinking: "I dare not destroy it. It's the only score in America." He put it back on the stand with considerable care and then continued his tantrum.

Toscanini's rehearsal methods were uncommon, the rehearsal itself at times being in essence a performance. He would usually go straight through a movement and then return to the points he wished to underscore. He would stop abruptly only if something was violently irritating or flagrantly wrong. Toscanini communicated with his hands, seldom speaking to us. In the first place, it was probably difficult for him to put his more profound thoughts into English. I have often remarked that I could put down on two sides of a piece of legal-sized paper all he said in the four years I attended rehearsals. He didn't have to talk. His hands and gestures were eloquent enough.

His involvement with everything he conducted was striking. And not every cloud engendered a storm. His conducting configurations were instructive, eloquent—albeit economic—and "gave ample room and verge enough" to weave his spell. Physically he was remarkable. I previously mentioned his skin. For a man in his seventies, he had an uncommon epidermis. There were no visible wrinkles, his skin very smooth and almost translucent in quality. The bone structure would have fascinated any painter or sculptor; and, to be sure, it did fascinate many. His eyes had that peculiar look that myopic eyes so often have: they appeared to be focused on something miles away, while at the same time turning in on themselves. He had a rather short, very powerful torso, and his legs were longer than one would have expected in a man of his height.

There were, of course, some things that especially seemed to pique Toscanini. Stupidity was one. He could not tolerate stupidity. He would rarely call down anyone for an initial lapse; but if the person made that mistake a second time, Toscanini's baleful expression, complete with gathered brow, was the signal that a tantrum was brewing. The third time, convinced the person was inexcusably stupid, he would begin to rage. He was equally irritated when he asked someone to play more quietly at a certain point if the musician responded, "But it's marked mezzo forte." Attempted homicide was in the offing at that juncture. He knew perfectly well, of course, what the indication was, but he wanted the passage slightly quieter, and no backchat!

Lack of emotion in playing angered him. How one member of the orchestra in particular (a wind soloist) stood up under the Toscanini attacks for years, I don't know. He was a fine technician, but there was no "blood" in his playing. Toscanini would admonish him, "You must put a drop of blood in each note"—quite trenchant, powerful advice.

Sometimes a person's face would rifle him. Though he was myopic, he could see certain things quite clearly, and he could not tolerate a face he regarded as stupid or brainless of aspect. He would persecute that man in a most unfair fashion.

It was my good fortune to have been asked several times to appear as soloist with the maestro. For instance, the first time I played *Harold in Italy* was with Toscanini. It is my understanding that all performances by the maestro were recorded and kept in the archives, and some of these were publicly released by RCA. But for some reason I was never able to fathom, *Harold* was not issued. The following year I played and recorded it with Koussevitsky and the Boston Symphony.

Some time later I was invited to Toscanini's house for dinner. The door was opened by a servant, but the maestro was there in the

95

hallway exclaiming very excitedly, "I have something for you, Primoroso!" (He always called me "Primoroso.") "I have something for you!" All through dinner he would stop in the middle of a sentence and repeat, "I have something for you, Primoroso." I thought that was all to the good, but, oh, how I did wish he would produce whatever it was—check, medal, testimonial, whatever.

After the meal we settled in the living room and he ran a record. Now, he was very vain about his shortsightedness, and only in the greatest extremity would he resort to wearing his pince-nez. He put on the record in his shortsighted manner, and the first two or three revolutions were just a fiendish scratching, scraping, and screaming. But after the needle settled down, I recognized *Harold in Italy*. Furthermore it was the performance that I had engaged in with him. I recognized it as such because Koussevitsky started at a slower tempo and built a gradual accelerando to the entrance of the solo viola. Not so with Toscanini. He started exactly in the tempo he conceived to be just and held it throughout the introduction.

He called me over after the first movement, patted me on the cheek, and said, "Poor Primoroso. I heard you with Koussevitsky. Poor Primoroso." Now if I had been the first to mention Koussevitsky on that occasion, he probably would have torn the wallpaper from the walls. He just couldn't tolerate his Boston rival.

Koussevitsky, on the other hand, never betrayed the manner of the *grand seigneur*. He was a rare character, diverting and engaging. He could have become the coronet and ermine and could have entered the House of Lords without hindrance, so lofty and aristocratic was his bearing.

On one occasion I was supping with him at his home in Tanglewood when an inept person asked him what he thought of Toscanini. The answer was revealing, showing how much these conductors love each other. Koussevitsky leaned back in his chair with a sort of puzzled look on his face and his quizzical, inimitable smile and repeated several times, using the Russian word for yes, "Da, Toscanini, da, da. Toscanini a great (pause) *opera* conductor." That was a droll remark, with the caesura perfectly timed. Beecham referred to Toscanini as "that little Italian bandmaster." Conductors are funny people—"kittle-kattle," as we call them in Scotland.

I recall an occasion when we were assembled in studio 8H of the NBC building to record the Beethoven Eighth Symphony. We had played no more than sixteen bars when Toscanini stopped and called to Charles O'Connell, who was then in charge of the RCA

Primrose, a favorite "Harold" in Italy

Red Seal Division, "O'Connell, do we have recordings of the Beethoven septet we made last week?"

"Yes, Maestro."

"I like to hear them now."

The entire orchestra sat for over three hours and listened to takes from the previous week. You can imagine the consternation; yet nobody ventured a word to recall him to the task in hand. RCA had to pay us three union hours and three lots of overtime, and most of the first desk men were getting either double or triple scale—and not a note recorded! Nobody dared to say, "Maestro, we're going to have to record the Eighth Symphony."

To be a really outstanding conductor one usually has to be dogmatic and unequivocating in what one does and set on the belief that one's way of doing things is the only way. Sitting as close to Toscanini as I did for four years, observing his face, symbolic of the inward spiritual force, I believed without qualification that everything he did was uncontestable. After I left the orchestra and listened to him as a member of the audience, I was no longer as certain, for I could see only his back.

He was indeed a very great conductor, but there were others. He was distinctive in his own way, just as Stokowski was distinctive. I would never fail to recognize a Stokowski performance, because of the sound. The sound he produced from an orchestra is unique.

I do believe that Toscanini was overglamorized and that he was not the "great" musician he was made out to be. This, in my opinion, was fortunate. For with a few exceptions the "great musician" conductors emerge as animated musicologists. Toscanini was a superb musician; but if it came down to a closer examination, I think other musicians would have outshone him—Bruno Walter and George Szell, for instance. As far as I am concerned, both these men had a much greater theoretical and musicological awareness of the subject. In this respect Toscanini reminds me a little of Warwick Evans, my colleague in the LSQ: each was a pragmatic musician with an overwhelming instinct for music that rarely betrayed him.

Toscanini perforce conducted from memory, but in this respect Mitropoulos would have outranked him. I remember Heifetz, who likes to have things accurate with no frills or nonsense, saying when someone claimed to know the Beethoven concerto backwards, "All right then, play it backwards!" Mitropoulos would stop while rehearsing works of great complexity, call out from memory a rehearsal letter, and then ask for a certain number of bars *before* the letter. Indeed he knew the work backwards. Toscanini always had the score handy. He would hold it up in that inimitable fashion of his, about two inches from his eyes, and count out the bars.

Working with all these conductors was vastly interesting. Stokowski, for instance, had a little trick to confound the orchestra, which I soon caught on to. He would stop, start counting measures to himself, command something like "Seventeen bars before C!" and then chide, "Why not ready?" This was a rather silly thing to do, since we had to count before we could play. But I soon "rumbled" him. I watched his mouth very closely. He would count forwards or backwards, and I would watch his lips as he counted to himself and have my viola ready. He could never quite figure this out—or perhaps he did but was not disposed to flatter my ego by mentioning it.

All these conductors have their "little tricks" to impress the orchestra—and it's very difficult to impress a hard-boiled orchestra, especially one from New York. But Toscanini did. Toscanini impressed everyone. He was much loved by some of the members of the orchestra and reviled by others. There was never any doubt, however, about the respect in which he was held, largely for his musical integrity.

Some people complained that his repertory was not extensive and that he conducted very little contemporary music, but I don't know if it was a valid complaint. After all, he was seventy years of age when he came to the NBC Symphony and could hardly be expected in the natural course of things to be a proponent of, or carry the torch for, contemporary music. Stokowski, of course, was conducting contemporary works long after he reached that age, but he specialized in this all his life, long before Toscanini wielded the symphonic baton. Koussevitsky likewise.

Toscanini just didn't care to involve himself, and the few contemporary pieces he did conduct were not worthy of his genius—Ferde Grofé's *Grand Canyon Suite*, for example. When he did conduct the *Grand Canyon Suite*, however, he made one feel it was the most important piece of music ever written. No music he conducted was to him insignificant.

My orchestral experience benefited me considerably, especially when I played concertos with orchestra. I know there are many soloists who won't pay the slightest attention to the conductor and who place the entire responsibility of the ensemble on the conductor's shoulders. But, knowing the problems of the conductor, I always observed him while I was playing a concerto. There are certain moments—for instance, the short and rapid ritardandos in the Walton concerto—that are manifestly difficult to negotiate. If one places the responsibility entirely on the conductor at these moments, obliging him to follow the soloist, the transient moment can become unstable. I would invariably suggest, "You direct the ritard. I'll follow you, and the orchestra will also. Then we're bound to be together." That's among the many things one learns from playing in a symphony orchestra.

The knowledge I gained from Toscanini himself was vast, but I must repeat what I have mentioned earlier: there was very little of this knowledge that I had not already heard from Warwick Evans in my formative years as a member of the London String Quartet. I believe the greatest influence the maestro exerted on me and on the orchestra as a whole was his insistence on clarity. Every note had to *sound*. He did not allow even the slightest excuse for untidy playing. A friend described it graphically: "When Toscanini conducts a work, it's almost as if one has gone into a vacant, unused room where a certain amount of damp prevails, walks up to a large wall mirror where the reflection is dim and imprecise, and wipes it clean. Suddenly everything becomes clear."

Toscanini had a profound influence on every musician who came his way. Some violently disagreed with his way of conducting, but others—the majority—agreed *in toto*. Winthrop Sargeant, who also played with Toscanini in the old days in the New York Philharmonic, pointed out in one of his lucid writings in the *New Yorker* the strong influence that Toscanini has had on music in recent years, with regard to precision and exactitude in following a composer's instructions in the score. He observed that there were others, contemporary with Toscanini, such as Furtwängler, Mengelberg, and Koussevitsky, who did not adhere to the composer's apparent intentions. The first time I heard Koussevitsky conduct the Ninth Symphony he warped a phrase in the last movement and I felt he should have been cast in jail. I was, as I believed, justly indignant and pretty sure that if Toscanini had been at the performance he would have been jailed himself for assault.

The point is, following Sargeant's argument, that the other conductors I mention began conducting symphony orchestras when they were young men and they became affected by a certain tradition that was rife at that time. Toscanini, on the other hand, became totally involved with the symphony orchestra at a much later period, after a brilliant career in the opera house. He had not come under the influence of this tradition. He was making his own traditions. He austerely believed that if a composer did not indicate a ritardando no conductor should have the temerity to make one of his own (though tradition had ordained that it be indulged in).

Many years ago I played with Frederick Lamond, one of the great pianists of the day and a revered interpreter of Beethoven. He was of the old school, which allowed the left hand to strike a split second before the right hand in order that the chord be endowed with the proper emotional content. Lamond's distortions of the music I performed with him were unconscionable as we understand things today. But the pendulum is never still, and it is quite possible that it may swing back to the pre-Toscanini era and enter again into a more romantic way of playing. As a result of this realization I now find myself much more tolerant of other people's interpretations than when I was in the orchestra, constrained by Toscanini's influence.

I have found that certain conductors who did not enjoy the aura surrounding Toscanini are especially effective collaborators or accompanists. I had not only esteem but great affection for the late Sir John Barbirolli and Sir Malcolm Sargent. They were such "comfortable" people to work with, as was not always the case with Beecham—and I have already commented upon my first performance of the Walton Concerto with him. Sir Thomas, unless he really felt in the mood, was not an ideal collaborator. He was too much the individualist. Besides Barbirolli and Sargent, who were the best I ever worked with, there were many other excellencies. No soloist could ever forget an experience with Sir Adrian Boult.

Incidentally, I think that unless a conductor has an enormous talent and authority he is likely to have a very rough time with an orchestra. No one can be more cruel than an orchestra player or an assembly of orchestra players if they are unimpressed with the conductor. No group can so easily kill a career—and that right from its inception—if its members as a body decide not to cooperate.

As an orchestra musician I became aware of a tradition that I came to denounce: the undue emphasis that is put on sight-reading ability at orchestra auditions. I thought this tradition a particularly senseless one with regard to the NBC Symphony. Here we had an orchestra that played one concert a week after about seventeen hours' rehearsal. The members of the orchestra had very little else to do, and hence not one of them was so pressed for time that he could not take his part home and study it.

I auditioned a number of violists with Rodzinski, and on several occasions he needlessly excluded applicants whom I perceived were able performers, his reason being that they couldn't read at sight. "Look," I pointed out to him, "these players are the type who are much more likely to take the viola part home than the smart-aleck sight-readers, who, you may find, will put the viola in their locker at the end of a rehearsal—and that is the end of their effort. It's a shame to lose some of these talented performers only because they don't read speedily." Surely there's no orchestra in this country so overworked that the players don't have time to practice a few hours on the side. If a player doesn't wish to, that's his business—until he is found out and properly dismissed.

In Great Britain in the early days the situation was quite different. The British orchestra player had a worldwide reputation for being an expert reader. Indeed, he had to be; until the BBC Orchestra was formed, the notorious and iniquitous deputy system prevailed, which allowed a player to call upon another musician to substitute for him if he had a better paying job elsewhere. In this connection the celebrated story is told about Koussevitsky conducting one of the London orchestras and insisting on five rehearsals—unheard of at that time. But he got his way. At the end of the fifth rehearsal he went to the principal bass player and congratulated him for being the only member of the orchestra to have attended all five rehearsals. The bass player then replied, "That's right, maestro, but I won't be at the concert tonight; I've another job. Me substitute's comin'." English players had to read like a streak if they were going to play Henry Wood's Promenade Concerts with one rehearsal for a different program every night for about ten weeks.

But this has never obtained in the United States. A student of mine, a very talented boy, auditioned for an opening in the Minneapolis Orchestra and was rejected because of his alleged inability to read at sight. A few days later he auditioned and was engaged by the Pittsburgh Orchestra. It gave me more than trivial satisfaction to inform the personnel manager of the Minneapolis Orchestra that my student hadn't had the slightest difficulty impressing himself on the demanding Mr. Steinberg. I also offered my opinion of this witless custom of judging a musician's ability and worth as an orchestra member on his skill as a sight-reader.

That sight-reading skill is indeed a poor index to musical talent is amply demonstrated by the case of a student I had at the Curtis Institute, a boy from Texas who had been refused entry as a violinist at his audition. His distraught mother made such a commotion when he wasn't accepted that the authorities, wishing to escape the vials of her wrath, persuaded me to take him as a viola student. They would! Any port after stormy seas.

At the termination of his third year I counseled this young man: "This is a cockpit of a profession you're in, lacking not a modicum of swinishness. I hope you realize that. You'll encounter a crowd of tough people who ape humanity so abominably, especially if you aspire to the orchestra world. Why don't you go back to Texas and find yourself a nice ranch or an oil well or something else rewarding? You are too nice a person to be in this profession." (Of course I was laying it on passing thick in the hope of diverting his steps to more auspicious and gracious avenues.) He was grievously upset and begged a reprieve of one more year. In the night of despair faith in light is admirable, as Rostand almost said, so hastening to the unmatchable library at Curtis, I extracted every notorious passage of viola symphonic music that experience had taught me he would most likely be called upon to read for an unoriginal, staid,

Primrose and Charles Munch

stuffy committee of auditors. He worked sedulously for the entire year and etched in his memory that path through the traps set to waylay the heedless aspirant.

Of course shortly thereafter he acceded to a sinecure. It wasn't long until I was asked by a well-known conductor if I had anyone to recommend for a vacancy. I sent this student to him. He later called to tell me, "I'll take him. He is not an out-of-the-ordinary player, but I've never encountered anybody who could sight-read like that!" That's why I think this business of reading is absolute nonsense. If a person plays well, if he has a serious approach and is obviously a good musician, snatch him! A person like that is usually soberminded, scrupulous, and will not neglect the duties expected of him.

The "game of chance," as Szigeti so acutely called it—the contemporary fad for competitions—is another manifestation of our musical scene that induces my disapproval. Unfortunately these competitions are a major force in today's musical world and in my judgment are an obstacle to that relaxed maturing so necessary to the young artist and the development of his repertoire. Nevertheless, they do present certain attractions. A young player of great ability can earn a goodly sum of money if he wins and can gain a reputation without having to spend a penny on a recital. In my time, in order to gain recognition one had to incur the expense of renting a hall and newspaper advertising and then preserve the fervent hope that by some adventitious chance prominent members of the press might be assigned to review the performance—in a favorable light, of course. One also hoped for some sort of audience who would come to listen to an unknown. Today if a fledgling player happens to come under the wire first in a big-league *passage d'armes,* he does not, as in the past, need a manager. The manager needs him! It has been my experience, however, that with few exceptions the fever of publicity so induced abates and the disillusioned victor retires into a vast, unbottomed limbo.

A further grave malady provoked by the competition fad has been the emergence of what I am disposed to call the "competition performer." The competition performer differs from the regular concert performer in numerous ways, ways that I believe are too subtle, too technical, to discuss in a book of this sort. A new breed of performer has developed, and one is prone to guess that a goodly number of these gamblers place their bets according to the recordings they have listened to. It used to be said among us chess aficionados that the man with the largest chess library was the man most likely to win a correspondence tournament, and I have a well-founded suspicion that the youngster who has the largest collection of the recordings of the *morceaux imposés,* plus, of course, the equipment to present them to the jury, is likely to romp home the winner. Szigeti tells us how somberly Bartók regarded these competitions, saying that competitions are for horses, not for musicians.

An obscure teacher may suddenly burst upon us like a hitherto unsuspected comet among the stars when one of his accredited pupils wins a prize in a competition of repute and distinction. Immediately a horde of aspirants to fame and fortune descend upon him, as hypochondriacs hasten to a doctor, be he quack or legitimate, who is reputed to have discovered a cure for what has been regarded as incurable. It is more than probable (indeed I have first-hand evidence of it) that the student was well prepared to win the competition before venturing to the phrontistery of the string Socrates.

Having won a competition, the young player immediately becomes known as a student of so-and-so, despite the fact that, apart from natural talent, most of what has been assimilated has been fed to this fortunate one by another teacher years before (in America perhaps half a dozen teachers, because no American student ever thinks of placing himself in the hands of but one professor). The teacher must be cognizant of the gins and snares awaiting the contender: the politics involved and the likes, dislikes, and prejudices of jury members. In many cases this type of teacher has himself been a member of a jury and has first-hand knowledge of such things. He will scrutinize the list of jurors and use the knowledge he has gained to the end that his entrant will be so many jumps ahead of another who is not so well advised. It is not a novelty to point out that the Russians win most of the prizes. They come sumptuously prepared to face the ordeal. They come as an assembly of inter-affiliated boonfellows, each supporting the other, although combatants for the paramountcy. They carry off the top honors, return to their homeland, and except for a few I do not know what happens to them thereafter. They have added to the glory of the Soviet Union. It is more than likely that none of them would have been allowed by the authorities to embark on such a run for the money if the authorities had concluded that they would, in any way, have blotted the escutcheon of the hammer and sickle.

*American tenor Richard Crooks, the man on the
north side of the street*

8

Richard Crooks and Others

I had been with NBC for four years when I began looking for a new position and fortune brought me to Richard Crooks on the north side of 57th Street in New York.

Dick Crooks was the best type of colleague one could have coveted. My cellist friend Lauri Kennedy had toured with another famous tenor years before—and Lauri really had been an *assisting* artist. If he contrived to elicit applause sufficient to warrant an encore, his principal became prim of mouth, grim of brow, and Irish of temper. Richard Crooks, however, would attend in the wings, particularly at the commencement of our initial tour, and advise me not only what to play as an encore but what to play to prompt a double encore. He gave me a great deal of advice about appearing before a public of his sort, which was quite different from the public for whom I had played serious chamber music or sonata recitals. They had to be handled differently, and it proved to be a significant education. This first tour accomplished, I did four more with Dick.

A remarkable thing occurred the following year at the first concert of our second tour. It took place at the old Philharmonic Auditorium in Los Angeles. We were staying just across the street at the Biltmore Hotel. Night had descended and I was dressing for the concert when I looked out of the window and observed the marquee. I saw in the announcement for the evening's entertainment that our names were in letters of equal size. I also noticed on the programs at the concert that it wasn't "RICHARD CROOKS assisted by William Primrose," but "RICHARD CROOKS AND WILLIAM PRIMROSE." Dick never did say anything to me about it, but I found out much later that he had insisted that the billing be this way.

As to the format of our joint programs, Crooks opened with an aria from the oratorio repertory—"If with All Your Hearts" from *Elijah,* for instance. I then followed with an alleged Nardini concerto, actually for violin, transcribed for viola—not a notable piece of music but suitable for this type of program. I must confess that I didn't have anything like the wide repertory I now have; I was just beginning little by little to gather music together to suit the occasion. Dick then ended with a group before intermission. The same sequence of appearances made up the second half, when I would play a group of short pieces—Kreisler or Paganini, for example. Dick usually finished the program with a group that incorporated several songs with obbligato viola, which I would improvise for the occasion.

Incidentally this was not the first time I had shared the spotlight with a tenor. I don't recall how I got involved in the concert in the first place, nor can I remember why it even took place, but I appeared once with John McCormack in, of all places, Dublin, Ireland. As an insignificant member of a debased strain of the Celtic race known as the Scots, I didn't receive much attention there that night. Irish whiskey was flowing freely and it was the Irish for the Irish. And the Scots? Who knows?

During our four years together Dick Crooks was an ideal collaborator. Here and there I received offers for solo engagements, which I accepted. I believe Crooks kept informing my proximate manager, Arthur Judson of Columbia Artists, what sort of success I was having and how the public was reacting to solo viola. The solo viola was faring very well. I also made many appearances arranged by Community Concerts when Ward French was in charge. I have already described in connection with the LSQ the tremendous boon this organization was to both artist and audience throughout the country.

Ward French attempted to form a similar organization in Europe and also in South America, but it was something that could only happen in the U.S. I was told that French and his "salesmen," so to speak, were very enterprising individuals. They would go into a town, find out who the prominent local musician was—organist, voice teacher, or what have you—and enquire if there appeared to be interest in a series of concerts sponsored by a nonprofit organization. If interest was evinced, Community Concerts would move in to demonstrate to them how to run the concerts, print the programs, and supply the artists. The profit that accrued to Community Concerts was taken from the artist's fee. For instance, if an artist commanded $1,500 per concert, which was a lot of money in those days, the parent organization would pay him $1,200 and the balance would accrue to Community. Some artists objected to this strenuously, but they, like so many others, usually had no head for business.

The value and usefulness of the Community Concert idea was that the artist had a ready-made audience, trimmed and tailored for him. He didn't have to go out and seek it or build it up on his own. He was also left with enough independence to play "straight dates," where he received his full fee. Ward French and his associates in New York were very anxious to have the program tempered to the shorn lamb. They wanted nothing to creep in that might put too great a strain on the "mid-American" listener's ear. Some of us tried to prove that this was wrong, and in some cases we did.

At first Ward suggested that one thing I certainly should do was talk to the public—tell them what a viola is, and so forth—in other words, make myself a real entertainer. This I did for a while, but then I became bored and no longer conformed. Another obligatory principle was that the accompanist should play a group of solos to add variety to the occasion. He would present himself halfway through the program and play the obvious Clair de lune and other such entremets, and these would elicit much applause. But it was against my grain; I didn't approve.

Over a period of some fifteen years I endeavored little by little to inject a better type of music into my programs. Permit me an example from my 1955-56 season. I opened with a Vivaldi sonata in Dallapiccola's realization, followed by the Bartók concerto. My accompanist then played a group of Mozart, Poulenc, Liszt, and other piano pieces of high quality. The final group consisted of one of my own transcriptions, the Andante and Hungarian Rondo by Weber, the Milhaud Sonata on 18th Century Airs, my transcription of the

Notturno and Scherzo from the Borodin quartet, and the Finale from the Concertino by Jean Rivier, a program of some merit. For a straight date I offered the same Vivaldi sonata, the Bloch suite, the Brahms F minor sonata, and the complete Jean Rivier Concertino.

My impression from my present vantage point is that this type of recital, or the type of recital program that was in its effulgence in the days of Fritz Kreisler, is on its way out. What seems to engage the public now is the group attraction. Pianists and some vocalists still attract, but very few violinists can draw a satisfactory audience unless they perform with orchestra.

If the solo recital is indeed approaching its demise, I would hesitate to hazard what the outlook may be for talented, career-minded young violinists. To what degree the careers of such as Perlman, Zukerman, and Laredo will attain, I can't really prognosticate. Since the demise of *Musical America*, I find it rather difficult any longer to follow the solo appearances of these young people. To be completely materialistic about it, I doubt very much if these youngsters will ever induce the fortune of Elman, Kreisler, Heifetz, or Isaac Stern. I think Isaac is probably one of the Last of the Mohicans in that particular sphere of performance. Even his career is different. I think he has probably made it as concerto player—the type of concerto player who every year performs with the same orchestras to the same adoring public, such is his popularity. He hit a spot, or there was one made for him—his aim was pretty accurate—just as a spot was made for me in the solo viola business. And I don't believe it can happen again. As do meteorologists, I believe that lightning does not strike twice in the same place.

The type of program I played in my day is finished; I'm sure of that. I know attempts are being made to make the recital more imaginative and communicative: the quasi-lecture recital, the part chamber music recital, where a number of other musicians join the featured artist.

A change of taste in music has very definitely come about, as it has in literature and painting. I think the emergence of rock music has had a lot to do with it. The young feel they have inaugurated their own type of music and they're not interested in the music that is dispensed to them by the Establishment. I am not saying they are right. I personally detest their music, not because it's a novel experiment or because it's an expression of youth, but just because of the sheer damned noisiness of it.

I fail to see any artistry in rock. There must be some, but it evades me. I don't understand why there is this urge for tre-

110

mendous noise without any variation. It keeps on at the same number of decibels without change, without surcease. It is so loud at times that I can't hear whatever melody there may be implicit. I don't know why noise should be loved solely for the sake of noise. Rock manifests something, something to do with this day and age, and nerves and the tension of living. I feel sorry for people who have to express themselves in this fashion. Using the word in its real sense, I find rock to be a rocking, shocking experience.

On the other hand, I react in a much different manner toward jazz. Of course people of the younger generation will point the finger and exclaim, "Yes, when you had what you wanted, it was okay." But surely, if I'm arguing just from the point of view of the noise, the range of dynamics in good jazz playing is immense. One of the most entrancing, fascinating, and delicate pieces of jazz playing I know of is a recording of Duke Ellington's with piano, double bass, and rhythm. It's done extremely quietly in Ellington's inimitable style, with the bassist, who is a superb virtuoso, playing pizzicato throughout.

I have heard from concert managers, men who have been in the business for a long time, that rock has made a big dent in ticket sales for regular concerts. Undoubtedly the convenience of television in the home has also contributed to the decline. I also think that the symphony orchestra is in danger of becoming extinct. I would say that thirty years from now the picture will change entirely, if a picture still exists. When I examine the scores of my former colleagues at Indiana University—Iannis Xenakis and John Eaton, for example—and see what they call for in the way of instrumentation and what they expect to hear, I find that it has no connection at all with the symphony orchestra of today. That music will require an entirely different type of player, one who will have to learn all over again.

I asked Xenakis what the response had been from the orchestras he has conducted. He said that at first it was very negative, almost a revolt; but once the musicians became used to his scores they started to achieve a new kind of technique and became involved. I would imagine that if in the future we want a really expert avant-garde orchestra, the players will have to be trained from a new conception. How they are going to overcome the string problem is something that escapes me.

I thought for a time that I should take a certain amount of responsibility upon myself to train young players to play avant-garde music. But when I look at some of the indications in the score and see instructions for playing quarter tones or sixteenth tones, which can be done with the slightest realignment of the finger, I ponder how, if somebody's finger is much more slender than somebody else's, is there going to be unanimity in rendering what is asked for. Our fingers are barely slender enough to play our own diatonic scales. If the score calls for an entire string section to play in micro-tones, the hazard will naturally be compounded. I don't know how this can be standardized, but perhaps it can. Perhaps our traditional string instruments will be supplanted by other instruments. As far as I've been able to discover, the avant-garde composer is simply not interested in string instruments as conventionally played. He's interested in them only for the peculiar effects he can elicit from them.

I do not regret the direction in which avant-gardism seems to be taking music. I think that change is inevitable, and when one begins to despair, then the closing days are upon him. We mustn't keep harking back to the past, believing that only ancient things were of good report. I don't feel entirely pessimistic about the future of music at all. It is going to be different. I can't pretend to understand it, but I'm certainly not going to close my ears or my option of understanding.

How our present string students will fit into tomorrow's picture, I don't know. They must go to the avant-garde composers themselves for the answer, or part of the answer at least. As long as we have traditional instruments, the students will have to be trained in a traditional manner. Actually I don't think these changes are very imminent. We don't have to abandon ship yet.

I have discoursed at some length about my career as a solo recitalist. With some disinclination I now turn to the playing of concertos with orchestras, the only aspect of my career that was a great disappointment to me. I received almost no invitations at all. People who now view me in the autumn of my career believe the contrary. They have the impression that I played with every orchestra in the country and frequently. I did nothing of the kind. I can easily list the orchestras with which I appeared: the Boston Symphony, Philadelphia, NBC, Chicago, St. Louis, Minneapolis, Los Angeles, Baltimore, Utah, Kansas City; and that's about it. Perhaps this seems a fair number of orchestras to have played with, to be sure, but in most cases they were first and last appearances.

When I was living in Philadelphia, I encountered Eugene Ormandy one day and he said, "I understand that you're going to be a Judson artist? As soon as you come under his management, I'm going to give you an appearance with my orchestra." He kept his word. I played the Walton concerto with him three times in Philadelphia and once in New York. As I recall, they were successful appearances, not only because of the public response but because of the press as well. But I never played with the Philadelphia Orchestra again. I've often thought I would have liked to point out to Mr. Ormandy that he might have done me a greater favor by not inviting me at all, because people were left thinking: Primrose has only played once with the Philadelphians and never played since. Why not?

Strangely enough, I have never played with the New York Philharmonic. During all the time I was under the aegis of Arthur Judson, who was also manager of that aggregation, I never appeared as soloist. I recall a friend of mine in the profession saying, "Why don't you go and sit on their doorstep? Make them engage you!" I said that I would do no such thing, protesting that "if I can't get in on my own merits, I'm not going to get in on my nuisance value." I did, however, occasionally suggest to the Judson office that I thought I was worthy of an appearance with the Philharmonic or that I had a new concerto (Bartók comes to mind!) usually written for me, and unlikely to sully the program. But I was invariably informed that the first violist wouldn't like it!

That sort of thing held true throughout the country. My several viola colleagues in the different orchestras very definitely played dog-in-the-manger. I suppose there was some excuse in the fact that, while the concertmasters of the eminent orchestras were accustomed to playing at least once a year, and sometimes the solo cellist also, viola players very seldom had an opportunity to appear in solo capacity. I suppose the solo violist felt that when the time came for a viola concerto to be admitted to the program he should be invited to play it himself. But the unfortunate thing was—and I make no bones about this—the performances were usually so bad that it was unlikely the concerto would survive the one performance.

In my judgment, very few of my colleagues in orchestras were capable of giving an adequate solo performance. Those who were capable will know; I need not suggest their names. Joseph de Pasquale, formerly of Boston and now with the Philadelphia group, studied with me for a short time while I was at the Curtis Institute. I can't honestly call him a pupil, because whatever magnificent qualities he had were his and I didn't have to teach him very much. I played with the Boston Symphony more than any other orchestra because they got into the habit of performing *Harold in Italy* (not really a concerto) and I was looked upon as their prize Harold.

Joe told me that if he had not been my student and if we hadn't been friends he, as solo violist, would never have *allowed* me to play with the BSO! "Allowed"!—rather astonishing, indeed. When other concertos were played, he played them, including the Bartók. I had commissioned the work, so you can imagine my discomfiture. I never appeared with the BSO in a "straight" concerto. I understand from a few gifted players of the younger generation, with lofty ambition, that they suffer similar discrimination.

I played once with the Chicago Symphony and that was that. I recall when the late Desiré Defauw was conductor he tried to explain the reason to me. Although he didn't say it in so many words, I got the impression that his solo violist wouldn't have liked it. I know that in San Francisco a similar attitude prevailed.*

This experience embittered me at that time, for I had worked very hard for the instrument and its promotion. When I was still with the NBC Symphony, I was told that I would not be engaged by other orchestras as soloist because of my affiliation with NBC. When I did take the risk of leaving the orchestra and venturing out on my own, giving up my orchestral career and my guaranteed salary, I expected that things would open up. The opening was as the eye of the needle. The situation in Europe, however, was eminently different. I could take off for Europe with all my new concertos and be given a royal welcome, and with no questions asked.

I have commented in a cursory fashion on that occupational hazard of stage fright in my remarks about the enormous battle Szigeti had to wage in this regard. Other performers have been affected by it, although perhaps not to that degree. I was affected from time to time by the malady, but not too often. It can happen for a number of reasons, but I would say that the prime occasion for nervousness is when one's conscience instructs that adequate preparation has not been made. I must confess to being nervous, not unduly, but definitely a little uncomfortable, just before my appearance with the Philadelphia Orchestra, my first appearance with an orchestra in many years. I had been playing either chamber music or as a member of an orchestra and hadn't played a concerto from memory in a

---

*In Honolulu recently, over a friendly lunch with Milton Preves, the distinguished solo violist of the Chicago Symphony, and his quite engaging family, he strenuously denied this circumstance, and his sincerity was undeniable. Nevertheless I never was engaged to perform the Walton concerto, the Bartók concerto, the Fricker concerto, the Milhaud concerto, the Porter concerto, or sundry others with this prestigious aggregation.

long time. The playing of such a complicated work as the Walton concerto was a considerable challenge.

What did scare the daylights out of me was performing the regular broadcast at the Academy of Music the day following the first live performance. There was no audience, and because of the exigencies of microphone placement I had to be three or four yards away from the conductor's podium. That might not appear to be a long distance, but it gave me the uncomfortable feeling that if I should have a lapse of memory I would not be able to glance at the score. I used to know the scores well enough to recognize where any part was on any page and to know where to glance in case of a memory lapse. A glance was sufficient for me, but I knew that twelve feet away from the score there was no such succor and I felt considerably nervous beforehand. This didn't affect my playing to any degree, however, according to the few people in the hall.

I was similarly discomfited at the premiere of the Bartók concerto, which I performed with the Minneapolis Orchestra. Antal Dorati is one of those conductors who pride themselves on their memory, so when it came to the first performance of the Bartók, which is not an easy work to memorize, Dorati arrived without the score. When I realized he was going to conduct it from memory, I really got the jumps. But again we got through it all right, and, as far as I know, my stage fright didn't detract from my performance.

I was flustered once in Toronto when I was playing *Harold in Italy* during the first half of a concert and, in the second half, Hindemith's *Der Schwanendreher.* During the long wait at the beginning of *Harold,* while the orchestra was introducing the "hero," I foolishly started to think about *Schwanendreher* and one particular spot that had always given me more than a little trouble. For maybe the second or third time in my career I started to shake. I began my long, slow entry in *Harold* with a most beautiful down-bow staccato, and soon everything appeared to be trembling. The concertmaster of the Toronto Symphony was an erstwhile student of mine, and my wife was in the audience. I felt ashamed of myself, but eventually the tremor worked its way out.

After the performance my wife and the concertmaster came backstage to congratulate me, saying they had never heard a more beautiful performance.

"What on earth are you talking about?" I exclaimed. "Are you kidding?"

They looked quite blank and said, "No, it was marvelous."

"But didn't you hear my bow shaking?"

"No," they insisted.

I couldn't believe they were telling the truth. I had been standing within a yard of the concertmaster, and I thought the seismograph up at Hudson's Bay would have registered the tremor. But, no, they insisted they hadn't heard a thing. This only proves the point I have tried to convey to my students when they have asked about stage fright. I continually assure them that unless there is an extreme on-slaught of nervousness it is heard only by the performer. Never-theless, when the bow starts shaking it is a disquieting experience—a paralysis of the arm over which the artist has no control. Moreover, as I never tire of repeating, only bad players are never nervous!

I suppose the anxiety of losing one's way while playing from memory is also a factor giving rise to nervousness. I tried not to let it get to me. I have found that the more you try to keep something like that repressed, the more it bedevils you. I must confess that lat-er, before I more or less gave up solo playing, with such com-plicated works as *Schwanendreher* I occasionally put the music on a stand, setting the stand low and slightly behind me, as a measure of reassurance more than anything else. Many times people didn't real-ize that I had music on the platform. An unseemly admission, I am persuaded.

The use of music during a solo performance disturbs me only if the artist stands four square to the rack and peers into the music, giving the impression that he hasn't taken enough time to prepare. As a member of the audience I expect him to take that time. One conspicuous example of the proper use of the music rack was in the appearances of Dame Myra Hess, unashamed and somehow unobtrusive. I have always decried the practice of a soloist playing a sonata by heart while the pianist is using music. There was the rather exceptional case of Szigeti and his son-in-law collaborator, Nikita Magaloff, who played sonatas and everything else by heart. Never was there a piece of music on the platform.

I simply tried to accept nervousness as part of the game. Some-times it can enhance a performance. It is only when it gets thor-oughly out of control that it is incommodious. It must have en-hanced my performance of *Harold* in Toronto if people whom I really trusted were sincere in saying how decorous the opening sounded. Frankly I thought it sounded like a bunch of marbles being thrown into a bucket. When we consider the tremendously exalted type of concert played by an internationally known artist and that he plays almost continually to very sophisticated audiences

116

in the largest cities of the world, we come to recognize the very great responsibility that is his.

I will admit to having included fare in my programming that was light and charming but trivial—the *Jamaican Rumba* by Arthur Benjamin, for one—and for a reason. The average audience will respond to that type of selection much more readily than to a Brahms sonata. I don't mean to imply that when I played Brahms it fell flat on its face—not at all. But the average audience reacted heartily to short, attractive pieces because they didn't have to listen too attentively. They were engaged by the charm of the work, and intellection was not demanded. One of the biggest selling records I ever made was *Humoresque* by Dvořák, with a souped-up orchestral accompaniment, and Nevin's *Rosary.* I grow uneasy when I think of these things today. But my, how they did sell! Fortunately I didn't often have to play such unedifying pieces.

I was engaged to play *Harold in Italy,* supposedly the violist's *pièce de résistance,* more often than I care to recall. It was once listed as the required work to be played in a competition with other instrumental concertos at Indiana University, where I taught. It and works for violin, cello, and piano had been decided upon by the various faculty chairmen during my absence from the university. Upon my return I protested to the string faculty in writing regarding this viola "concerto":

The assumption that Harold in Italy *is a viola concerto, and worthy to be ranked with the works chosen for violin, cello, and piano fills me with dismay.* Harold *is by no stretch of the imagination a concerto, in my opinion. It is very much a symphony, and stands or falls according to the skill and musicianship of the conductor in charge of its performance. The demands on the soloist are: (1) a fine instrument, or the type of player who can make any instrument sound impressive, and (2), perhaps the most important demand, the performer's gift as a Thespian: the ability to stand, as in the last movement, for ten minutes looking handsome and urbane without in any way being vulgarly obtrusive, or distracting attention from events taking place in the orchestra. Furthermore, how does one go about teaching it? Fingerings and bowings I could suggest, and if a student asked me to prepare him for a performance with Toscanini, Koussevitsky, Beecham, or Munch, I could do so, and the reason is obvious. However, unless these performances are to take place in the hereafter, my guidance would be of little avail.* Harold in Italy *is in no sense a test in the manner that a true concerto should be, other than a test of one's financial status as to the choice of an instrument, and of one's stagecraft. The fact that I made a career of it*

117

*was fortuitous, and a freak hardly likely to be duplicated. Good
luck, like lightning, rarely occurs in the same place twice.*

Personally I think that when Berlioz discovered that Paganini wasn't
going to play his piece he gave up after the first two movements as
far as the violist is concerned. A fact? Not at all. A frivolous assumption? Yes.

Despite hard work and careful preparation I have found that it is
impossible for a soloist to play at his optimum at every appearance.
Often it is extraneous things such as towns, halls, audiences, and
hotels that either enliven or dampen a performance. I remember
once that David Stimer, my accompanist, and I arrived on a grim
morning in a grim town in Pennsylvania. It was raining torrents. We
were met by a grim individual who was head of the society which
had engaged us, were taken to a grim hotel, and sat there looking
out of the window at grim rain pouring down on grim surroundings.
When we arrived at the auditorium that night, we found that the
grimmest place in the building, the so-called artists' room, had been
reserved for us.

We played our regular program, and there was little applause for
anything. I thought, "When we come to the *Jamaican Rumba,* we'll
certainly get them then," because that piece always evoked a repeat. But it didn't this time. As it turned out, I barely scraped in one
encore. I went back to the artists' room and said to my accompanist, "David, we flopped tonight." Then the grim gentleman who
had met us at the train that morning came backstage and announced solemnly, "Gentlemen, allow me to tell you that this evening you had a triumph." We were stunned, and I said, "Well, I'd
hate to be here on an off day!"

One learns in time that there are certain places where people
more or less sit on their hands with a sort of "prove-it-to-me" attitude. You can depend on other audiences always to respond; they
appear to enjoy what they are listening to unless it's too obviously
bad. From a soloist's viewpoint, much depends upon the audience.
To return to the grim town in Pennsylvania, if it had happened that
the audience that evening had been a lively one, other things might
have been forgotten; but everything was of a piece. In many in-
stances where I found a dull audience, however, I may have been
only prejudiced, for one doesn't know how much of the response is
due to myself. It's like the case of the English tenor who had been
singing in Huddersfield and said, "What a marvelous town Huddersfield is!" He approved of Huddersfield. But when he was que-

ried by his friend, "Did you ever sing in Hull?" he answered, "Yes, and what a miserable hole it is!" Obviously he had had a success in Huddersfield but was panned in Hull—and there is very little to choose between. Hell, Hull, and Huddersfield, according to an English aphorism.

As to countries in general, I found very responsive audiences in Germany. I have already noted in Italy the audiences were charming and delightful to play for, but they chattered all the time, especially the afternoon audiences. That was probably because I was an instrumentalist; it wouldn't have happened, perhaps, had I been a singer. London audiences were warm and knowledgeable, but in Scotland they tended to be the "prove-it-to-me" type.

I think two places I particularly enjoyed were Munich and Cologne, where the audiences were sophisticated and the *ambiente* inspiring—the *Herkulessaal* and the hall belonging to the *Rundfunk*, respectively. Because the environment can be such an important factor, I mention a few other halls. The Festival Hall in London is rewarding, especially considering that the platform at one time was no more than one or two feet above the floor level, conducive to a very intimate feeling between artist and audience. The old Queen's Hall was a gem, as was St. Andrew's in Glasgow, which has since burned down, and the old Salle Pleyel in Paris, which also burned down. I seem to have played in quite a few halls that later burned down. I don't know the reason for that, whether I should feel ashamed or unique. In this country several halls are outstanding: Clowes Hall in Indianapolis, Symphony Hall in Boston, and the San Francisco Opera House—all rewarding to the performer—and, of course, Carnegie Hall.

I must say that when I toured the United States I became quite accustomed to the amenities of the tour—after-the-concert parties, for example. If a reception of some sort was not held afterward, David and I felt like orphans of the storm. Invariably there were parties, and some extremely funny things took place. Once in a southern state we were driven quite a way out of town to a home that had all the appearance from a distance of the sort of house Charles Addams depicts for the *New Yorker*—mysterious and forbidding. In the course of the evening the hostess asked what I would care to drink. Since I was in a southern state, I felt it appropriate to request bourbon and soda. "A what?" she queried. "Bourbon and soda, please," I repeated, not knowing that it was *de rigueur* to ask for bourbon and branch-water. A mysterious, protracted hiatus elapsed before she eventually brought me a tray with a bottle of

WILLIAM PRIMROSE
Violist

DAVID STIMER at the Piano

PROGRAM

I

Concerto in B flat . . . . *Vivaldi*
(Realization by Dallapicolla)
Largo — Allegro — Largo — Allegro

II

Sonata (1939) . . . . *Hindemith*
Breit mit Kraft
Sehr lebhaft
Phantasie leading to Finale (mit zwei Variationen) leicht bewegt

INTERMISSION

III

Notturno, Opus 42 . . . . *Beethoven*
Marcia Allegro
Adagio
Menuetto
Adagio — Scherzo
Allegretto alla Pollacca
Variazione — Marcia Allegro

IV

Concertino . . . . *Rivier*
Allegretto rustico
Adagio molto cantando — Allegro — Vivace

BALDWIN PIANO

Program of a typical Primrose-Stimer recital

120

bourbon, a can of baking soda, a spoon, and a glass. I tried to explain to her that I had wanted a club soda. "Oh," she said, "I'm so sorry. I thought perhaps you had indigestion."

Of course on occasion there were some people who could be annoying and who would keep pestering by letter, telephone, or personal visits at concerts. But I was usually able to brush them off without being rude about it, I think. I didn't have a retinue at any time. Unfortunately I was never a great diplomat backstage. By that I don't wish to imply that I was unkind to people; it was just that after a performance I wanted to depart as soon as possible. I used to admire Victor Babin enormously in this respect. He behaved with a courtesy that was redoubtable toward backstage visitors, no matter how strenuous the concert might have been. Even the most crashing bore would be courteously received and his questions, however witless, answered, very often eliciting Babin's own considerable wit.

Whenever children were present in the audience, they would come in droves backstage for autographs. I would try to sign their programs as rapidly as possible and that is why my signature is almost illegible. I reduced it to about three actual strokes of the pen—not far removed from Japanese cursive kanji:

An example of the sort of question that would have annoyed me, but did not, because of years of exposure, was once posed by a mother after one of my concerts: "Why do you play with your eyes shut?" (This is actually a fairly common habit among soloists.) Before I could answer, her little son piped up and said, "Don't ask dumb questions, Ma. He's scared to look at the audience."

Then there was the inevitable question that cropped up in every interview: "Can you tell us exactly what is the difference between a violin and a viola?" I usually gave a serious answer, explaining the difference in pitch, size, timbre, volume, range, and so forth. However, on one occasion a mischievous imp took possession of my tongue and I replied, "The difference between the violin and the viola is that the viola is a violin with a college education!"

I had some moments of embarrassment during my concertizing, which more often than not were moments of crisis. At such times I

121

felt a curious sensation of distance. I had a sense of being outside everything, looking on. If, however, the situation became intense enough, I was wont to giggle inwardly—a reflex of some sort. Hysteria? I used to be very much afraid that my giggling would become audible, as it nearly did at one appearance with a top orchestra in the U.S., under a very distinguished conductor.

I was playing the Bartók concerto, a work of some complexity. We had had adequate and very profitable rehearsals, and during the concert everything was proceeding smoothly. At a certain point in the first movement—measure forty-one, to be exact—the conductor for reasons of clarity, safety, and convenience should subdivide the beat. This conductor was proceeding to do so when some misunderstanding arose between him and the orchestra. Immediately everything became disorganized. The orchestra got out and perforce tried to get back in, but the result was chaos, confusion, and heartbreak. I could hear a little toot on a flute, a tentative scrape on a cello or violin, and the conductor, drenched with perspiration, anxiety, and dismay, desperately calling out bar numbers. My reaction? The whole thing struck me as being so ludicrous that the ill-suppressed giggle took charge. I knew that an orchestra *tutti* was approaching and that at that point the status quo would be reestablished. My accompanist, sitting in the audience, was in a panic. He was sure that the whole thing would come apart. *My* only fear was that I might start laughing outright.

Afterward the conductor was very apologetic, but I told him not to grieve about it at all. We had gotten through all right, and as it was a first performance of the work with his orchestra few, if any, could be completely certain that things had come unstuck. This was proven by laudatory comments in the newspaper the following day. A leading critic, who quite understandably had never seen the score and who knew that Bartók had the reputation of being an *escamoteur*, remarked upon the extraordinary "meshing" of the solo viola and orchestra during this section of the first movement. I said, "You see? Nobody guessed. If the critic had known, he would at least have spelled 'meshing' as 'm-e-s-s-i-n-g' and have been much closer to the truth!" The incident struck me as immoderately diverting. Without that outrageous sense of humor, my whole performance might have collapsed.

Embarrassing things did happen, but I don't especially want to forget them. Before I came to America, I went on tour with a very famous English singer, Dame Clara Butt. Dame Clara was known all over the British Empire; she was almost like cricket. At her concerts,

she wrapped herself, sometimes physically, but at all times emotionally, in the Union Jack. She was very much loved by the musically
untutored because she gave pleasure instead of instruction. She had
the most unusual voice with an uncommon range. She was in turn
mezzo, contralto, and sometimes baritone. She didn't try to blend
the various ranges. The change of registers was very definite and
occasionally disconcerting. This particular tour took us to Dublin in
the Irish Free State. Dame Clara's husband, Kennerly Rumford, was
also a singer, and he shared the program with her. At the end of
each performance the two sang the national anthem, "God Save the
King" (as it was then). This song has three verses, unknown by most
people, that are unabashed doggerel. She would sing the first verse,
he would sing the second, and the audience would be expected to
join in the third—a regular jamboree. She insisted on doing this in
Dublin, of all places, and the president of the Free State was in the
audience. A few people stood up, but of course not the president.
It was unprecedented, very embarrassing, and extremely hazardous.
But nothing—no plea, no admonishment, no appeal to reason—
would stay Dame Clara's determination to manifest her patriotism
and her loyalty to His Majesty. I thought she stood a good chance
of being lynched. Such are the intimations of nationalism, which, as
I mentioned earlier, I deplore.

In those days it was my obligation to play the national anthem on
the viola, and the audience would invariably join in ("Sing Along
with Primrose"?), which leads to an extremely amusing story about
Richard Crooks. On one of his early visits to Canada—as he told it—
he was informed that he would have to sing the national anthem.
He objected, saying that he didn't know the words. He knew only
that the music was the same as "My Country 'Tis of Thee." "No
problem," the manager assured. "You needn't worry, because when
you start to sing the audience will immediately stand up and join
you." So Crooks sang, and the audience did stand up—but they
were so anxious to hear his voice in real life, the voice they had
heard so often over the radio, that they *didn't* join in; they simply
remained silently at attention. Poor Richard didn't know what to do,
so he simply repeated, "God save our gracious King, God save our
gracious King, God save the King. God save our gracious King...,"
and so on. He wanted to make quite certain that the king was going to be saved because he couldn't do anything else.

I was with the NBC Symphony on a South American tour when,
as the story goes, Toscanini pulled the orchestra out of bed early on
July 4th to play "The Star Spangled Banner." It was just before

America came into the war. And when France was overrun, it was Churchill, I believe, who suggested that England and France should in effect become one country and shore each other up. In the orchestra we played around with the possibility of naming this new nationality the "Fritish" or the "Brench." This, of course, was a little childish, but it did offer some relief to those of us who were British or French at that dire moment. When the news broke that Mussolini had stabbed France in the back, Toscanini abruptly left his table in the dining room and strode to his cabin, his face blanched with fury and grief. We didn't see him for two days. I'm told his stateroom was wrecked—by himself.

Then one night I had quite a start aboard ship. At that time a neutral ship—an American ship such as ours, for example—had its national colors painted on the hull and was also floodlit so that it wouldn't be torpedoed by marauding submarines. On that particular night, for some reason I cannot explain (for I usually slept soundly, so unblemished was my conscience), I got up and looked out the porthole. The spotlight wasn't functioning, and our flag was *not* there. Oh no, I thought, any moment now! I hollered for the night steward, who hollered for his superior, and so they went hollering on up through the bridge of command, and we had our light and flag functioning in short order. It doesn't sound like much now, but at the time I experienced a decided *frisson*.

During the war years one accepted certain inconveniences on tour. It was often difficult to get a pullman reservation, and we got used to lying down wherever we could find space. I very often slept in the luggage rack at the end of the car. I was once told what must have been one of the great comedy routines in the history of the pullman berth: Piatigorsky in an upper berth with his cello, trying to disrobe, in what must have looked like an exhibition of all-in wrestling.

At this juncture I want to pay tribute to my accompanist of so many tours in this country, David Stimer. I have played with many pianists, including Ivor Newton, Franz Rupp, Gerald Moore, and other greats. David, however, was my constant accompanist, collaborating with me for over seventeen years. He was connected with one of the radio stations in New York and was recommended to me by an acquaintance.

When David and I met, I was due to leave the following week on a South American tour. My previous accompanist was a Belgian national and unable to obtain the necessary visas for the Latin Ameri-

Primrose in the 1950s

can countries we were to visit. A considerable brouhaha ensued, and I was at my wits' end until David came to the rescue.

As I had to broadcast a program to that area beforehand, I thought I could really test my new accompanist. I gave him my music one day prior to the broadcast and told him we would rehearse at the studio and then perform. He played so exceptionally well that I was confident my troubles were over—and they were.

Stimer was a wonderful person to tour with and a very good chess player to boot. There is nothing like chess to take up the slack in protracted journeys. He was a natural at it, having never studied a book. I was also a fairly good player at the time, but I had read many books and had taken lessons with a Grand Master. Otherwise David would have beaten me with ease. He had the chess brain; I had a good memory. Our interests were sufficiently varied that we didn't feel obliged to demand each other's company constantly. In addition to being a very fine musician, he was also a very well-read man. Short and stout, with an interesting and sensitive face, he had also an enjoyable wit and a scalding sarcasm when his sensitivity and sensibilities were affronted.

Each fall when we would begin our tour, David invariably appeared to have lost weight after a summer of dieting. Hence, when we started out he was light and so was his suitcase. But as the tour progressed, he proceeded to put on weight—and so did his suitcase. In every town we visited he made a beeline for the local bookstores, record shops, and good restaurants. He was constantly amassing rare and out-of-print books and records and had an impressive collection of both. By the time we got to the end of the tour, his suitcase was strikingly heavy and he was filling his clothes very well indeed. As the English so delicately put it, David was "a man of full habit."

I don't believe I ever entertained any thought that I might one day be touring the world as a viola virtuoso. As I said earlier, I simply wanted to play viola much more than I ever wanted to play violin, and I had made some solo appearances in England and Europe before I came to this country. I have also mentioned that certain aspects of my career were poorly managed. Despite this there were those fortuitous events that aided my career. There was the inestimable benefit of the early recordings, the Paganini caprices, and later those with Heifetz and with Feuermann. Those were gratifyingly successful, as was the recording of the *Humoresque* and *The Rosary*, of which I was much ashamed, by the way, because of the meretricious quality of the music. And, above all, my fortuitous meeting with that rare human being, Richard Crooks. There couldn't have been a more fortunate concatenation of events. I think my life's work has been one continual progression. There is, of course, no good reason not to mention the fact that my progress has been hindered by a condition most everyone knows about—the trouble I have had with my hearing. That, plus the severe coronary I suffered some years ago, more or less put an end to my concert career. But my knowledge of music now is much greater than it was twenty years ago and I am also a much better teacher. My fingers, peculiarly enough, seem to be moving with even greater ease than formerly, although they could move very rapidly then. I have never had any trouble keeping my left hand limbered up and certainly no difficulty with the bow, because handling the bow, thanks to Ysaÿe, became second nature. It's like riding a bicycle or driving a car or flying: once you've got it, you never lose it.

I did not have any set plan so far as my career was concerned. I knew what I wanted to do, but I felt it was best to go step by step and take up what came my way. I just tried to do the best job I could possibly do at the moment and then hoped that something else would emerge from it. As to concertizing, I enjoyed everything connected with it: the performances, the travel, meeting new people, seeing new places and old friends. Because the jet age has set in, it is, of course, possible to be in a different country within only a few hours, with its different customs, food, language, and culture. All of this has been a very great delight to me.

A pensive Primrose

9

Critics

I always felt that when I received a good review the critics were astute and well-informed. If the review was adverse, they knew nothing. I have had my share of both, and I must admit that, at the time at least, the unfavorable ones rankled, especially if I thought I had performed well. An artist feels that a bad review is unjust if he has really given a program a great deal of preparatory thought and attention, only to find it given a curt dismissal. Whether the victim is justified in his conviction is, of course, something else. I tried to take no notice of abuse, but it was not always easy.

Different artists react in different ways with regard to critics. When I joined Heifetz and Piatigorsky in a concert in San Francisco some years ago, one reviewer, obviously out to make his name by assailing the mighty—a ploy of minor scribblers—wrote a scathing, scurrilous article on Heifetz's performance. I was so angry in his behalf that I was quite convinced we should all pack up and leave. But Heifetz doesn't do that sort of thing. He stayed at his post, not the least bit put out, and continued in his faultless way.

Years ago in an early appearance in London at one of the smaller halls, Kreisler elicited a good review in the *London Times*. That same day Jan Kubelik, who was at his zenith and lionized by the public, played in the Albert Hall. Kubelik was given about three-quarters of a column, unfavorable. Kreisler attracted the other quarter: appreciation and respect. His manager, after reading Kubelik's uncomplimentary review, said, "Look, Fritz—look what Kubelik got, and look what you got!" To this Kreisler replied, "I would rather have had the big bad one," meaning that it was more important to have three-fourths of a column under any circumstance—a remark not unlike that profound philosophical comment attributed to Mae West: "It's better to be looked over than overlooked."

Some, like the late Ernest Newman, who was respected, though apprehensively, by everyone—at least British artists—give much delight to their readers in dispensing scathing sarcasm and shrewish witticism. But I hold that it is much easier to contrive the studied insult than to play the right note at the right moment in the blink of an eye. A sample of Newman comes to mind. During my student days in London I was engaged by the wife of a renowned Harley Street doctor to "assist" her in her annual vocal recital. She was a singer, of sorts, and doubtless the eminent surgeon sought to gentle her now and then with the gift of a public appearance. He must have had some pull with the press; otherwise I'll never understand why, or how, Newman came or was assigned to the concert. At any rate, here is what he had to say about the recital the following weekend in the *Sunday Times*:

Miss _____ gave a recital at the Aeolian Hall on Wednesday night, assisted by Mr. William Primrose, and a few friends in the audience.

Tout court!

Two critics I personally admired, among a few others, were Neville Cardus and Irving Kolodin. I came to know Neville tolerably well but was always uneasy in a way, because I never cared to become too intimate with a critic.

Our friendship actually burgeoned from a common love of cricket; we rarely discussed music. Indeed, Neville had devoted a good many columns of praise and derogation before we formally met at lunch at that Mecca of all who savored the sumptuous board, Pagani's, the unmatched restaurant a hop, skip, and jump from the Queen's Hall, both destroyed in the holocaust of the London blitz. The talk quickly turned to the humor to be found in the bowling of

Grimmet, the nobility of Wooley at bat, the identicalness to Kreisler of Sir Jack Hobbs wielding the willow, or of Heifetz to Sir Donald Bradman.

Neville's reviews of cricket and cricketers were as profound and perceptive, and couched in the same gracious prose, as his reviews of music. He was at one time a professional cricketer. But throughout his life his passion was music. It disturbed and perturbed him that thirty years ago he was much better known as a writer on the game than as the leading music critic of the *Manchester Guardian*. We frequently watched and discussed the contests together, but he didn't allow this friendship to interfere with his musical criticism.

When an Australian cricket fan took Sir Neville to task for all his musical allusions in his reports and admonished him to write more about Hobbs and less about Schnabel, Cardus rejoined by admonishing his critic to read his musical contributions during the winter season. As a stylist Cardus had few peers and a wealth of tradition. All who served the *Manchester Guardian* while the sublime C. P. Scott occupied the editorial chair had to be men who knew how to put proper words in proper places. Hazlitt was the fount of Cardus's critical acumen and Burke the fount of his felicitous turning of a phrase. Though it seems such encomiums must today be distributed with niggardly hand, it was not so in the time of Cardus, and I think he would have agreed when Dr. Johnson told us that in his day nobody talked much of style since "everybody wrote pretty well."

To my knowledge, little good has come of a professional musician's attempting to assume the role of the critic. Apart from a handful of the professional journalist critics, the residue are barely worth printer's ink. That there have been some captivating and perceptive pencrafters contributing to our various news media requires no stressing. Indeed there have been and continue to be—especially those who vouchsafe their several opinions to the Sunday periodicals when they have had a week or several days at least to think things over, as distinct from those galley-proof slaves who have but a few hours or less to meet a deadline.

James Huneker was perhaps the first of the truly notable musical journalists, although I am baffled to perceive how he managed to write as much as he did and preside for such interminable periods at Lüchow's *biertisch* (his favorite bistro), as is alleged by such of his cronies as H. L. Mencken. Mencken declares in his revealing essay that on one occasion when Huneker was in full flush of his middle years he joined him for lunch at one o'clock and provided

H. L. M. with the most amazing monologue his ears had ever funneled into his consciousness. The waiter was then—it was now six o'clock—hauling in Huneker's tenth (or was it his twentieth?) seidel of Pilsner.

After Huneker no really great figure appeared on the musico-journalistic scene until the era of Newman, Cardus, Harold Schonberg, and Kolodin—or so, as a critic of critics, is my confirmed judgment. These gentlemen, though they may not have penned their opinions on gargantuan draughts of the malt brew, wrote an exuberant and provocative prose, and, so far to the good, Schonberg and Kolodin continue the elegance of the tradition.

Schonberg appears to have discarded the scaffolding of many of his less gifted contemporaries and lifted himself above the general. He does not wallow in dogmatics and appears to abhor the hollow tosh of disparagement and pejorativeness, refusing to tarnish his pages with it. He gives me the impression too that he is a professional musician rather than a musico-journalist. I have no evidence that he has ever been a practicing musician in any branch of the art, but even with such Titans as Ernest Newman, Cardus, and Huneker himself I have always decried the stigmata of the amateur, using the word in its most complete sense: the votary. Though I cannot trace the literary or stylistic ancestry of Schonberg, I can never be deceived.

When the London Times was an anonymous sheet—when it did not afford its contributors a by-line—Cardus was recruited to substitute, during the England cricket team's quadrennial visit to Australia, for the regular cricket correspondent, the aristocratic and somewhat overwhelming "Beau" Vincent. I, a regular reader, was in America at the time and, having been deprived of the scuttlebutt, was not aware of the change. I had not read more than the introductory paragraph of the initial report from Perth, however, when I said to myself: That's Neville. When Schonberg reported the shenanigans between Spassky and Fischer from Reykjavik, although the New York Times was not so coy as its London counterpart, I did not have to hesitate for a moment to recognize the source of the article and the hand of that most diverting contributor: he had so much wit and mirth and so much chess acumen.

It may seem from what I have written on the subject of critics that the gentlemen I have just mentioned were consistently kind to me in their several judgments. Not a bit of it! I got "a bit of stick" from all of them and, like most of my colleagues, resented the scourgings at the time. However, time and reflection have healed the wounds and I am wont to consider that in many cases their strictures were merited. And, above all, they were masters of their *métier*. I am reminded at this point of a comment that rended the air at Madison Square Garden in the golden days of Joe Louis. I was in my usual ringside seat watching every move of the stalking, shuffling "Brown Bomber" who never wasted a motion (unlike today's jumping-jack Muhammad Ali). Suddenly, as was to be expected, his wretched opponent—although a pretty good scrapper in his own fashion—left a tiny opening in his defenses and "swifter than the arrow from the Tartar's bow" came the inevitable left hook and right cross. Needless to say, his bucko was lying inert on the ring floor. There was an almost sentient gasp from the assembled witnesses to the execution and in the moment prior to the wind and fury of acclaim came this unforgettable sanction from one of the fans: "From the Champ it's a compliment." So when I reflect on Cardus and other masters I have mentioned giving me their "bit of stick," I am compelled to agree with the commentary.

It is my recollection that a certain critic for a now-defunct Gotham journal reviewed me only three times (I never subscribed to a press-cutting agency or kept a press book), and he disapproved of me on each occasion. For that matter it seemed to me that he disapproved of everybody who was of high account. It was well contrived, an old-fashioned gimmick: iconoclasm. It well suited his editor to have a covey of distinguished musicians waiting to skin his contributor with blunted knives on every other sector of West 57th Street. Little did he care if he, "like wanton boys that swim on bladders," was a honeysweet dapperling of musical incompetence. In his diatribes, he called it humor when he gibed. He had much epicene wit and spleen about him. I think there is no more sordid episode in the American musical chronicle than the many orchestras and conductors, during this critic's incumbency, laying up for themselves the base treasure of a kind word in his columns, by affording him opportunities to foist his corn-belt hymnody through the medium of his glee-club-stick-wielding directing of their various orchestras thus debased. Not infrequently, with shrewlike viciousness, he bit the hands that fed him. All this apple-polishing subsided as quickly as he relinquished his job.

After my recital in New York, which, from the reaction of the public, was an unequivocal success (after all, I had accomplished the impossible as a violist: a sold-out audience in Carnegie Hall and a seven-encore recall), the same critic fired his poisonous darts of bootless uncordiality in his column the next day. Though the remainder of the New York press was equally disapproving, it was hardly so venomous. (It is strange how this sort of thing may happen from time to time—a unanimous disposition to denigrate a performer or a composer. But it does, and one should not suspect collusion. It would be just too farcical to conceive the gentlemen of the press meeting in the bar at Carnegie Hall and agreeing, "OK, boys, let's give him the works.") A week later, with considerable trepidation, I approached another New York appearance with Toscanini, when the whole picture changed—the status quo was reestablished—and I was restored to my former position as one of the "fair-haired boys" of the critics—all except one, who paid but the most grudging admission that Toscanini and Primrose, while apparently acceptable to the public, were still not acceptable to him.

I received a column once—and I won't mention the source—that tempted me to make physical retribution for what I felt to be critically abusive commentary. But I constrained myself. I am aware, however, of incidents in which restraint on the part of the artist was actually thrown to the wind. There was the case of Albert Sammons. The story has it that a certain critic in London reviewed his concert adversely. This particular critic belonged to the old school; he was a dignified gentleman who always turned up at a concert in his Prince Albert and top hat, who lived in fastidious fashion in a "nice" suburban villa.

After reading the review, Albert went to this critic's house, applied the brass knocker, and was greeted by a trim little maid. "Is Mr. So-and-So at home?" Albert inquired. Being assured that he was, he went on to say, "Tell him that Mr. Sammons would like to see him." She ushered him into the drawing room and announced that her master would see him as soon as he had finished his breakfast.

Eventually the old gentleman came in with all his dignity and said, "Good morning, Mr. Sammons. And what can I do for you?"

"Is your name So-and-So?" Albert asked.

"Why, yes, it is, Mr. Sammons."

Then Albert rose up in his wrath and in his inimitable cockney accent said, 'Well, the next time I see you at one of my concerts, I'm going to come down off the platform and knock your bloody 'ead off!" Albert was indeed down-to-earth, honest, and unequivocating, especially in certain situations, albeit this story may be apocryphal!

I mentioned earlier the famous English singer, Dame Clara Butt. Her husband, Kennerly Rumford, also a singer, was the personification of a guards officer—handsome, debonair and with his guards mustache rampant, his bearing, and his speech. At one concert Dame Clara received a scandalous review and so her husband did what only a gentleman, a clubman, and an Englishman could do. He attired himself to suit the occasion as he understood it, with cutaway and top hat, an Ascot tie with impeccable tiepin, and a dog whip. He waited on the steps of Queen's Hall until the critic appeared, whereupon he seized his man and publicly whipped him. There are sundry ways of handling critics.

The Heifetz-Primrose-Piatigorsky Trio at the Pilgrimage
Theater, Los Angeles

10

Colleagues

I have always been very skeptical when I have found a human being elevated to a sort of godhood by his admirers. Casals, one of those musical luminaries I have already mentioned whose memorable performances have stuck with me, is one of those people who came under my scrutiny because of this very thing.

I played only once at Prades. During the first part of the concert I sat in the audience with Isaac Stern, whom I joined in the Mozart Concertante later in the program. Casals played, as was inevitable, a Bach unaccompanied suite. Of course his audience was in a state of utter ecstasy after the first bar or so. Isaac turned to me, "Well, isn't it something—the greatest!" I answered without any double meaning, ill feeling, rancor, or anything that you might regard as unworthy, "That's the best damned seventy-five-year-old cello playing in the world!" What I meant was that if I, upon reaching the age of seventy-five, could play my viola as he played his cello that night I would indeed be proud of myself. But I was not going to admit that it was the greatest cello playing in the world. I didn't think Piatigorsky was out of the running, or Fournier, Rostropovitch, Starker, or other cellists of repute. I felt they should not be excluded from the realm of all the far-stretched greatness.

My feeling about this in all branches of music, and other things as well, is patent. I am hesitant to put the label "greatest" on any person. I believe that this is perhaps something inherent in the American character—this proclivity to label and categorize things. The heroes in many fields are ticketed, and people seem to want this done in music too. They want to specify which is the greatest orchestra, the second greatest orchestra, the third greatest, etc. To me, this is all nonsense.

I have no way of knowing whether Casals resented or appreciated what his admirers and cohorts did for him; but what they did for him I found distasteful. A good friend of mine wittily and succinctly described them at this very festival at Prades as "people going around being 'gothic' about Casals." One understood what he meant—hands together in prayerful attitude, heads bowed. I thought it grossly unfair to his colleagues for the public so indecorously to elevate him. Now that he is no more, who is going to be Number One? Who is to be groomed for the position of the Greatest Cellist?

I would, however, not wish to be interpreted as denigrating Casals's contribution to the resurrection of solo cello playing. Not at all. What he has done for cello playing and cellists is beyond appraisal. Had it not been for Casals, I believe the younger cellists could not have done what they are doing today. By the same token, I and my colleagues in the viola world could not have done what we have done if it hadn't been for Tertis, who, incidentally, was the same age and had the same birthday as Casals. But I don't find anybody in Great Britain being gothic about Lionel Tertis. We all recognized him as a magnificent player in his day, and he continued to perform until he was heavy with years. If I had heard him in his last days, which unfortunately I didn't, I would have made the same remark: "I think he's the best eighty-year-old viola player in the world."

Now I sense that I may have painted myself into a corner because I was dubbed the "World's Greatest Violist." But I don't think I paid much attention to the title apart from the fact that it was used widely by my management for publicity purposes. It was Koussevitsky who bestowed this accolade, and if he was good enough to say what he did—and he commanded a certain respect

138

when he made public utterances—then I suppose there was no harm in the management's using his phrase and praise. When people protest that Casals or anyone else should be able to use *his* accolade for business purposes, I find it quite in order. But it seemed to go further than that in his case—and in other cases too.

In my own case I don't think I have ever been hero-worshiped, much less deified. But if a coterie ever starts canonizing me, I hope my reaction will be as it is now. If one lives long enough, honors come pouring in. It seems that the first essential is the accumulation of years. One has to have a lot of them. I suppose that's what riles the young people—aspiring to a place in the hierarchy. Generally speaking, I cannot put definitive labels on anything connected with music. It's much too diverse. I am reluctant to put an exclusive label on any person, event, or thing.

Even Jascha Heifetz, as great as he is, has not yet been deified in the sense that Casals was. My collaboration with Heifetz over the years in concerts and recordings stems from our first meeting in Mexico City in 1935. Quite a number of artists, including Heifetz and those of us in the London String Quartet, were gathered for the opening of the *Palacio de Bellas Artes*—that glamorous and ornate opera house with its tiffany drop curtain. As I recall, Heifetz played a recital at the opening matinee, the very first concert given in the hall. The quartet performed at the hour referred to as "vermouth," which is the cocktail hour, of course, serving to designate any concerts taking place around five o'clock in the afternoon. The evening concerts took place at 9:30 or 10:00 p.m., and one was fortunate to get out by 1:00 the next morning!

In the evening we all met at an apartment to enjoy a genial and relaxed party. Heifetz soon had us rolling on the floor with his remarkable imitations of *perfectly* bad fiddle playing. I realized then that to play *perfectly* badly one had to be a perfectly marvelous fiddle player. It is easy to burlesque, but to play perfectly badly is something else.

Years later Heifetz made a recording of a number of pieces he performed that evening, under another name for private issue. The record jacket displayed the photograph of a rather stupid-looking young man in full evening dress with a fiddle under his arm, bearing no resemblance to Heifetz whatsoever. Jascha played the record for Piatigorsky and myself at the end of one of our recording sessions, saying that it had been sent to him for his approval. We just stared at each other with a wild surmise. But, mark you, we kept remarking: This fellow is talented! No doubt about it. He must have been

Jascha Heifetz

very badly taught, yet he is talented. His fingers are remarkable in certain passages, but when he comes to a scale he misses part of it and ends up a half tone too high.

That evening, after I returned home from the studio, I began to reflect on the recording and remembered I had heard Heifetz do that same routine in the flesh. I was quite sure he had made the record himself. Later it turned out so and he gave me a taped version of the disc. Years later, at one of the audition sessions at Indiana University, after the string faculty had listened to applicants in person and had proceeded to tapes I put this one on, and the faces

Joseph Gingold, Primrose's colleague at Indiana University

of the faculty were just as puzzled as mine and Piatigorsky's had been, and the opinion was very much the same as we had pronounced.

The chairman of the faculty said, "I really don't think we can admit this applicant on a graduate basis, not at his age (which was given as twenty-two). He is too old for us to reorganize all this bric-a-brac, although he is apparently talented."

"I think you are making a mistake," I said. "I am sure he would do very well here."

And I was asked, "Would you accept him in your class?"

"No," I replied, "I am professor of viola, not violin. But I believe he'd go far. What about you, Gingold?"

"No!"

"Well, you're making a big mistake. That's Jascha you are listening to." The result: pandemonium and disbelief.

I suspect most people probably know Heifetz only as a rather cool and austere public figure and are not aware of his gifts as a comic, at least so far as it refers to his imitations of bad fiddlers. I don't know that he is a comic in other ways. He has his own peculiar brand of humor. He would probably be the first to agree that the much more entertaining colleague was Piatigorsky, who had a gift of storytelling that was in its own way unmatched. There was his *macédoine* of English with a very pronounced Oxford accent on certain words, interspersed, of course, with a Russian accent and a great wealth of imagery.

One of the greatest in this line is Artur Rubinstein. He has the gift of imitating dialects and miming that Danny Kaye would not disdain. He has an infinite charm and a high sense of humor. But I wouldn't say that Heifetz is a man of humor at all. He has developed this parlor trick—his perfect imitation of perfectly bad playing—but otherwise he seems to take things pretty seriously.

The only time I recall Heifetz ever being taken aback was many years ago when he was playing a recital in London. I went with a friend of mine, a viola player, but who resembled much more a guards officer in civvies. He was a handsome fellow, dark complexioned and tall, sporting a guards mustache, and always impeccably dressed, not forgetting his bowler hat and his tightly rolled umbrella. He would never have been taken for a musician. Though the general public often expects a musician to have long hair and be a little untidy, very few of the "stars" fit the description, at least forty years ago.

My friend was aware that I knew Heifetz and asked if I might take him backstage and introduce him. Heifetz, as ever, played the kind of concert that knocked one right back on one's heels, and it took a lot out of him. As we entered the artist's room, we found Heifetz leaning up against a table, a trifle weary. What followed was almost like a vignette from a P. G. Wodehouse Bertie Wooster masterpiece. I introduced my companion: "Mr. Heifetz, my friend, Mr. X, would so much like to meet you." Harry, completely overwhelmed and almost speechless with awe and nervousness and wanting so badly to express how much he had been impressed—nay, enkindled—by the performance, grabbed Heifetz's hand and feverishly exclaimed, "Jolly decent, old boy, what? Jolly decent!" I'll never forget that festive moment as long as I live.

In the mid-fifties the Heifetz-Primrose-Piatigorsky Trio was formed for recording purposes and worked amicably for the succeeding half-dozen years. In all the association I had with Heifetz, he never tried to dominate any musical situation. I never had the feeling that he was trying to impose his way and only his way. He would listen very carefully to Grischa, because he had the greatest respect for him. He listened to other people's opinions as well, and in every case if he didn't approve he expressed himself to that extent.

When Heifetz was playing string quartets for recreation with experienced people such as myself, Sascha Jacobson, or the late Sir John Barbirolli, who used to join us with his cello, he seemed almost to be *looking* with his ears, picking up all the different tricks of the trade and leaving no stone unturned in his effort to get to the bottom of the secret of that esoteric pastime.

I do recall one occasion, however, where Heifetz did become more than mildly insistent. When he, Rubinstein, and Feuermann were preparing to record the Beethoven "Archduke" Trio in California, I was on hand to take part in the recording of the Mozart Divertimento in E-flat and the Dohnányi Serenade. Those were the days of the 78-rpm recording, and at one rehearsal (when I was "dummy," so to speak) I was asked to turn pages for Artur, and to use a stopwatch to mark in the piano score four-minute, four-fifteen, and four-twenty intervals so that a choice of break could be made in the most appropriate and musically intelligent place. Granted, it was a rehearsal, and détente prevailed so that when they came to the last movement, with its jaunty, lilting theme in the piano, Rubinstein injected more than a modicum of Polish espiéglerie.

I was standing behind him, watch in hand, and he turned to me and winked. Heifetz just stopped playing, and everything else stopped. The stopwatch stopped. He didn't say anything at first, but faced Rubinstein and gave him the sort of look he reserves for the undue prankster. Then he said in a very precise, somewhat martinet manner, "Do you mind if we do that again?" Artur just shrugged his shoulders and "played it straight." With all my soul I wish Artur had insisted on his own version. I don't remember any other occasion when Heifetz imposed himself even to that extent.

There was one thing I might have resented at the time, but it rather tickled me instead. In some passages it would have been helpful if Heifetz had given some sort of lead, maybe with the scroll of the instrument. But he would not. In the Arthur Benjamin *Romantic Fantasy* there are some tricky cadenzas, tricky not only from a technical point of view but in the matter of ensemble.

I would ask him, "When we come to the recording, will we do it this way?" He would respond that he couldn't promise. And so I would protest, "I do wish you would at least give me some idea." But he would insist, "I really don't know. We'll wait until we get to the recording studio." Indeed he didn't tell me and indeed he didn't lose me, nor I him. It was a kind of try-and-catch-me-try-and-lose-me situation. I had such a vast amount of experience in ensemble playing that I think he knew it was going to be very difficult for me to come unstuck, but he'd try me anyhow.

If I'm allowed to boast a little, I would have to say that our ensemble playing in the *Romantic Fantasy* is rather good, commendably precise. And I don't wish to leave the impression that this all came about by accident. We did work hard—Heifetz always works hard—but we didn't slave ourselves. The cadenzas, however, were definitely an adventure, and in the recording I had to be on my toes. But Heifetz's extraordinary sense of rhythm, an almost implacable sense of rhythm, is very easy to follow—not to follow as the common locution has it, but to be with.

I believe our recording of the Mozart Duo, previously mentioned in these pages, is for me one of the finest examples of Jascha's playing, particularly the second movement. But then there are so many examples! Another that comes to mind immediately is the third movement of the Beethoven Trio in G Major, Op. 9, No. 1. This is an incredibly touching piece of playing—among his most moving. Heifetz never recorded the companion duo to the Mozart B-flat, the one in G, because he didn't like it. I assume that's going to be a lasting dislike. For years he wouldn't record the Mozart Concertante for the same reason, but eventually he changed his mind.

My first recordings with Heifetz were made when I was still in the NBC Symphony. What happened then makes quite a story. Heifetz recorded the Beethoven concerto with Toscanini. I was, of course, in the viola section of the orchestra and was genuinely touched and moved and filled with admiration at the way he performed his task. To play a work that demands so much from the soloist, with a conductor such as Toscanini who had a lofty reputation for his conception of Beethoven, and to play with such accuracy and virtuosity as he did that day, was no mean thing. It was a heroic occasion. I wrote to express to Heifetz how I felt—one of the very few fan let-

The Trio in concert

ters I have written. He didn't reply, but I did learn that he was rather touched.

Shortly after that he invited me to his home in Connecticut to play chamber music. We essayed, among others, the Dvořák piano quartet with Feuermann as cellist and William Steinberg at the piano. It was then that Heifetz suggested and we discussed the possibility of recording the Mozart Duo and the Handel-Halvorsen *Passacaglia*. Eventually we did record them and added later the Mozart and Dohnányi string trios with Feuermann.

The Trio spoofing, with expressions of mock seriousness

My relationship with Heifetz didn't go beyond what might be described as a congenial comradeship. I don't know all his friends in the profession, but I would say that his closest relationship was with Piatigorsky. No doubt this was because they are both Russian and contemporaries. I always treated Heifetz with the greatest respect. Among other things I learned early was the importance he attached to punctuality. I know I never missed an appointment with him and was usually five minutes ahead of time. I think this impressed him over the years, if nothing else did.

The trio itself was disbanded after some dozen recordings, sometimes with assisting artists in more extended ensembles. I would say this was mainly due to my hearing problem. Over the last couple of years of our collaboration Heifetz was very helpful, very considerate. But the time came when my inability to hear a particular section of the scale accurately became a matter of considerable moment to the ensemble. The actual break in our personal relationship I never could fathom. I had an idea what it might be, but I dismissed it as more than a little childish. However, this is one of the characteristics one encounters from time to time in people who have attained to greatness in other aspects.

Shortly before I left California to go to Indiana University, Piatigorsky and I dined with Heifetz at his beach house. We had a wonderful evening, and once again he gave his imitation of perfectly bad violin playing—a sort of parting gift, I assumed. Everything appeared to be in order, but later I was definitely conscious of a complete change in our relationship. I had no more contact with him and couldn't establish any. A year later I returned to California for the summer vacation and met him on the street quite by chance. He made it clear in no uncertain terms that he was considerably upset by my behavior. He "thanked" me for all the letters I had written to him. The irony wasn't very subtle, since in our long association I don't think we exchanged more than three or four letters. The few times I did write to ask his opinion about something or other, or for any other reason, he invariably made his comment at the end of *my* letter itself, put it in an envelope, and returned it.

When he accused me indirectly of not keeping in touch with him and not letting him know what was happening at Indiana University, I knew it was nonsense. It struck me at the time that he might have resented my departure from the teaching position that I had, along with himself and Piatigorsky, at the University of Southern California. But I felt that my life was my own, that I was in thrall to no man or situation. Moreover, I felt nothing very much was being accomplished there for a great number of reasons. I knew, on the other hand, that a great many things were being achieved at Indiana. I like to be active. I like to be surrounded by young people.

Heifetz might have thought I was ill-advised to carry the heavy load I did in Bloomington, but at USC the load was so light it was almost airborne. After some inquiries I eventually discovered that he actually did resent my leaving. He felt we had started something together at USC and I shouldn't have quit. In some ways that's rather touching; but at the same time he knew, and we all knew, that the situation was disintegrating. The special division that had been created for us just ceased to exist. That he continued teaching under various other auspices is something else again. I am extremely sorry that it had to end up the way it did, but there was not much I could do about it. I have made no subsequent attempts to communicate with Heifetz. I know my man well enough. Once he has made up his mind on a certain point, he's very unlikely to change.

I have not yet discussed my other associate in that trio—Piatigorsky. But then one could never discuss Grischa sufficiently. He

148

Gregor Piatigorsky

was too extensive a subject. I first met him in the early thirties but came to know him well in 1942 and onwards when we were thrown together as teachers at the Curtis Institute in Philadelphia. He lived on one side of Rittenhouse Square and I on the other, which reminds me of an amusing incident.

His wife, Jacqueline, is a Rothschild. At the outset of my recollections, I mentioned my noble "relative," Archibald Philip Primrose, Fifth Earl of Rosebery, who had three ambitions in life, one of them being to marry the wealthiest woman in Europe. He married a Rothschild. One day shortly after Grischa and Jacqueline were married, I saw, from the window of my apartment, Grischa walking in the square. So I went down, slapped him on the shoulder, and said, "Good morning, cousin!" "Vat you mean cousin?" he said. I tried to explain. The Rosebery connection is tenuous, to be sure, but it was enough to pull this little joke on Grischa.

I would describe Piatigorsky's playing as I would the man: expansive. He had an extraordinary breadth of sound and emotion—tremendously vivid playing. Heifetz, on the other hand, is a very reserved personality on the stage and rather aloof. From the moment that all six feet, four inches of Grischa walked on, carrying the cello above his head, you knew he was going to make a lively impression on the audience even before he put his bow to the string. I don't mean to say that Heifetz doesn't make an impression. He makes a very definite impression because of his most austere and aristocratic bearing.

Piatigorsky's gifts as a teacher are well known. He was a great teacher. His power of imparting was remarkable, and his imagery found a mirror in every mind. He never flagged and he never allowed his students to flag. They had to be *expressing* all the time.

An artist who has made a lasting impression on me is Yehudi Menuhin. Of his precociousness as a youngster and his matured artistry of later years I have been aware since my student days with Ysaÿe. I have heard Menuhin many times over the years, and most recently at Gstaad. There was a spiritual essence about his playing on that occasion which was most impressive.

As to other fellow artists, especially the violinists, my oldest friend among string players is Nathan Milstein. We met when he came to Belgium during the time I was studying with Ysaÿe and we have remained friends ever since. He lives in London now, so our meetings are few and far between. Our first weeks together were unusual as he had no English or French at that time. He spoke both German and Russian, but I had neither of those. When I met him some

150

To dear Bill, with the lifelong
admiration and affection of
Yehudi Oct, 1969

Yehudi Menuhin

years later in New York, he was speaking fluent English, French, Italian, and Spanish. I am sure the reason many artists from east European countries are so linguistically proficient is that few foreigners speak east European languages. We English-speaking people are completely spoiled, because no matter where we go someone is sure to speak our tongue. At first Nathan and I communicated only in a sort of sign language and in music. We would repair to his room or mine and for fun play, among other duos, arrangements of

151

Nathan Milstein

Haydn string quartets for two violins! Who arranged these, who published them, or where he obtained them has completely escaped me.

I have always thought of Nathan as one of the most extraordinary violinists I have ever encountered. His pragmatic knowledge of violin playing is vast, and I hope he will teach regularly someday.* Moreover there is a refreshing naturalness in his playing. I remember him at the home of that quite lovable true amateur—true in every sense and aspect of the word—Dr. Morris Cottle of Chicago, where we gathered for many an evening of chamber music. Between quartets Nathan could be caught leaning negligently against the chimney piece, a cigarette dangling from his lips, playing Paganini caprices all over the place. Once he starts playing, he is difficult to stop, I am happy to relate.

He believes in taking a commonsense approach to everything, doesn't make anything mysterious. Because of this characteristic he was once able to work out a troublesome problem for me. I had tried to inculcate in my students the idea of playing without a shoulder rest. But in my own convoluted way I had frequently left them completely puzzled as to how to go about it. I was apparently being too verbose, too abstruse. Milstein doesn't use a shoulder rest, which fashion he derived directly from Leopold Auer, who frowned upon its use. So I asked Nathan, "How can I explain to my students how to hold the viola without a shoulder rest? They're always worrying about dropping it and grip it like a vise between their chin and shoulder." Nathan said, "Tell them that's not the place to *hold* it. The shoulder is only a resting place. They must hold the violin with the left hand." So why not the viola also? This is eminently correct and a typical example of Nathan's impressively simple, commonsense approach.

I enjoyed a long-lasting friendship with Szigeti, having first met him at Blackpool in 1909. That was the occasion when I rather impertinently asked him his age, which he admitted was seventeen or thereabouts. I have played with him at various times throughout the years. The last great musical experience I had with him was in London in 1970, where I sat next to him every day for almost a week as a member of the jury for the Carl Flesch Competition. Listening to his opinions and criticisms of the competitors was revealing.

I am reminded of his insight regarding the fugue from the G minor sonata by Bach, one of the required pieces at the competition.

---

*It is well known that since this writing he has established himself as one of the violin's most outstanding teachers.

At the moment a series of chords occurs with the theme in the bass, many of the contestants whipped the bow back from the top, breaking the chords almost as inverted arpeggios. This irritated him immensely and he gave forth whispered invective. He felt, and I feel, that if the player can't play the notes of the chords as an entity he shouldn't be playing the fugue at all. It can be done quite easily if one has the requisite bow technique. Strangely enough, it takes a light stroke to accomplish it, not a heavy one, and no digging or scraping. Regarding performances of Bach unaccompanied works, I feel the player should be licensed, just as is a doctor or lawyer, before afflicting his listeners. In my judgment a mere handful of fiddlers is capable of adequate performance.

I always regarded Szigeti as a remarkable violin player. I have already spoken of the Edinburgh Festival and the intimidating battle he had with his nerves. There were times when his nerves overcame him and he occasionally missed a note or passage. But that happens to everyone, even Heifetz—that is, I have heard Heifetz miss things in rehearsal, but never in public!

Concerning this, Heifetz once complained that it was a terrible burden to be expected to play immaculately at every performance. "If I miss a note, everybody hears about it. If Kreisler misses a note, nobody is concerned." While I was teaching at Curtis, Heifetz performed on the Telephone Hour radio program playing the Wieniawski D minor concerto, in which, in the last movement, there is a great skip up to a harmonic B on the G-string. He missed, and the next day the students could talk of nothing else. They didn't remark about his movingly beautiful slow movement or the sparkling staccato in the finale, or all the other stupendous things he accomplished. All they talked about was the missed note. How dared he! And Heifetz's having missed gave them very good reason, so they thought, to miss also without rebuke.

Szigeti's last book, *Szigeti on the Violin*, is wonderfully illuminating, a book that every string player should read, along with the Carl Flesch autobiography, which includes Flesch's revealing and sometimes surprising opinions of his contemporaries. The one violinist admired without exception was Ysaÿe. I have yet to encounter a musician who, having heard him, had anything but the most exalted opinion of him. Whenever anyone of note passed through Brussels, he paid a visit to Ysaÿe's residence in the Avenue Brugman, somewhat after the manner of the pilgrimage to Mecca.

I had great admiration for Mischa Elman. He was out of a special mold; his tone was glorious, as recalled by all who heard him. A

For Bill Primrose
wonderful partner
in those *seasons* of
memory

1968

Josef Szigeti

Mischa Elman

wonderful incident has to do with this legendary virtue. Often after a concert an admirer will comment favorably about one's instrument, forgetful of the fact that without the artist—and dependent on his skill—the instrument would be dumb. On one occasion an admiring colleague—mark you, a colleague, who should have known better—was adulating in the most effusive manner Mischa's glorious sounds, saying, "Mischa, what a fabulous tone your violin has!" Becoming more than a little impatient, Mischa handed it to him and in his high-pitched, intense voice said, "Here, you play it!"*

Mischa's life was overshadowed by Heifetz, and he frankly felt that Heifetz was immoderately extolled. He loved to play chamber music, and we did a great deal of informal playing together. Some of his interpretations were, to say the least, curious. When Mischa got hold of a tune that had any kind of juice in it, he really got on it and squeezed it. He took tremendous liberties, which in the last years of his career he seemed to eliminate, rather as Stokowski did.

Elman's annual New York recital, the last one before he died in 1968, was to me an instance of what was taking place in the realm of the recital then. He played a handsome program that included a Handel sonata, the Brahms G major sonata, the *Poème* of Chausson, and a group of smaller pieces—the kind of program he had played all his life, the kind Kreisler and all the fiddlers of that era played. I was shocked when I took my seat in Carnegie Hall. In the first place the hall wasn't full, and secondly those in attendance represented the old faithful cohorts who had gathered around Elman for many, many years. Very few young people were in attendance, and I felt it was a great pity that the youth hadn't turned out to hear this man, who at seventy-five was still playing superbly.

The experience confirmed what I had been aware of for some time—the recital as we knew it during my time, the recital that I loved because I had been brought up on it, was on its way out. The younger generation is not interested. Elman was a bewitching fiddler, no doubt about it, and his death was a tremendous loss to the world of string playing. He should have been teaching too. He had a great deal to impart.

I lament the fact that Elman didn't teach. One thinks of such a violinist, having achieved his enormous artistry at such an early age and in such a genial and intuitive manner, perhaps being spared the consciousness and often the travail of systematic learning. Still I be-

---

*Most archetypical of Heifetz is the story related of a similar incident when the inept visitor to the artist's room elicited from Heifetz, bending his ear to his violin case, already tightly closed: "I hear nothing!"

lieve he would have been able to impart or to verbalize the process of learning to students. I admit, however, that when I attended Heifetz's classes, for example, ten years ago and more when we were colleagues at USC I got the impression that if a student had a difficulty it was beyond Heifetz's comprehension. He would play and adjure the student to "do it this way." But there are many students who just couldn't comprehend that kind of instruction, just couldn't "do it this way."

Since that time Heifetz has had a great deal more experience and no doubt his approach and understanding have changed. I know from my own experience as a teacher, which has been much longer than his, that one learns to impart as one goes along. You draw on your own personal experiences. That's why I maintain that the most valuable teacher is one who has played in public, who has gone through the experience and weathered the storm, either as soloist, orchestra member, or chamber music player.

Milstein, I believe, must be able to impart because he is so articulate, so sensible in his simple and straightforward approach to all fiddle problems. He and I discussed many technical considerations, and he always had an uncomplicated explanation. Kreisler did not teach, alas. It is a pity when these magnificent fiddlers fail to do so, for they should pass on their legacy to the next generation.

There are, of course, other violinists who have their own very personal styles. But when I try to describe the distinctive qualities of a series of fiddlers it gets almost to the point of satiety. It's like attempting to look at all the pictures in the Louvre in one day. I'm afraid that I will start using the same words all over again. Nevertheless I believe that Isaac Stern's most impressive qualities, for instance, are the vividness and ample warmth of his style plus his tremendous involvement. I have known him since the early 1940s when we made friends rather quickly, and we have remained friends ever since. His enormous vitality and vigor and his life of almost nonstop action are things to be envied. That he can keep going at such a pace fills me with awe.

I met David Oistrakh the night before his New York performance in 1955. We were both staying at the same hotel, but he had no English and his wife, Tamara, acted as interpreter. The day of his New York debut was a very big day indeed. In the afternoon Elman performed with the New York Philharmonic; then Oistrakh gave his recital around five o'clock with Elman and Milstein in the audience; and that evening Milstein played his recital with Oistrakh in attendance. Oistrakh was one of the friendliest people I ever encountered in the music profession. I got an impression from him of great sincerity and simplicity. He appeared to have no frills or fripperies of any sort. And though he had great dignity, he was still a very warm human being.

I was greatly affected by the playing of his son, Igor, when I heard him in Los Angeles—much more so than the press would have led me to expect. There was, of course, the inevitable comparison between father and son, and I do believe that Igor got more than the heavy end of the stick. I was deeply impressed by his playing and wrote his parents in Russia to tell them so, because I felt that they, like any parents, were bound to be anxious for their son's welfare and success in a strange country. David didn't wait to write back a note of thanks; he cabled me. I don't think that was a matter of P.R., rather just a manifestation of his innate courtesy.

And now for a few impressions of some of the violinists of the generation immediately preceding my own. I played quite a bit of informal chamber music with Carl Flesch in London. He is so well known as a pedagogue and theoretician of the violin that people are apt to forget he was a very fine solo violinist and chamber music player as well. I did, however, find his playing a trifle dry, as I find most German playing. This, of course, is a matter of personal taste. Huberman I knew but slightly. I was once recruited, as a member of the ensemble, to play the Chausson Concerto for Violin, Piano, and String Quartet with him in London, and I fully realize that it is just a blind spot on my part—for he was greatly esteemed by a host of admirers—but I never could enjoy his playing. As I recall, it was unlovely playing. To my ears, he scratched abominably. He was one of the great violinists that I would never go out of my way to hear.

I met Enesco only very late in his life, when he was badly crippled. I heard him play but once and didn't particularly care for what I heard. It is, however, most unfair to pass any judgment at all on one hearing when the performer is manifestly ailing. Like so many musicians, he could have had an off day to compound the problem of his physical disability. Thibaud I didn't hear very often either, but I remember his playing as being very refined and urbane. At that time, however, Kreisler was also at his apogee and, in my opinion at least, overshadowed Thibaud and all others.

My first recording of the Mozart Concertante was done with Albert Spalding. Charles O'Connell of RCA brought us together for that express purpose. Albert was a *charmeur*, a gentleman of aristocratic bearing, well spoken and well read. But I think maybe he was

To my friend William Primrose.
With admiration for his great art.
Albert Spalding —

Albert Spalding, eminent American violinist

a little overawed by the responsibility of being the only American violinist of prominence in his day. That was the time when American violinists, like British violinists, were not supposed to play well. That role was left mostly to the Russians, thank goodness, and to a few Germans, for which I was not so grateful.

Fellow artists influenced me as a performer in about the same way that I would imagine everybody is affected. There must always be something in the equipment of a worthy rival or colleague that commends itself to you, and if you are flexible at all some of these things are bound to be incorporated into your own playing. I have never tried to disguise the fact that Kreisler wielded a very strong influence on me.

Kreisler's inner rhythm, which is a difficult thing for people to create, was indescribable. At times during his annual concert at Carnegie Hall, if one looked down the aisle at people who had their legs crossed, one would see many feet swinging in time with Kreis-

160

ler's playing. Kreisler was one of the first violinists to use the kind of glissando that requires one to slide from underneath the note he is approaching. Heifetz does this in an inimitable way today. These and other mannerisms, plus their sounds, render Heifetz's and Kreisler's playing unique in our time.

From among the pianists I would include Rachmaninoff, Horowitz, and Schnabel in this group of inimitables as well. I find them easy to identify. If I tune my radio in the middle of a recording, I can guarantee to spot these five players every time. Regarding their individual tones, I don't think I could find words to describe them without resorting to a "penny novelette" sort of English. When other top-ranking violinists are playing, I can be momentarily confused and waver between choices: "It sounds like Milstein, or Stern, or perhaps David Oistrakh." But with Kreisler and Heifetz I am never in error.

Tone is so individual, so personal, as to render it very elusive of analysis. A few basics I learned from Ysaÿe concerning the bow may be the essence of tone production. One point concerning string crossing I have already dwelt on at length in my discussion of Ysaÿe—namely that one mustn't "crash" from one string to another. The stroke has to be controlled and firm and perfectly smooth. Allied with this is the absense of pressure on the bow. The pull comes from the weight of the arm, and this applies particularly to viola playing.

Many varieties of vibrato should enhance what the bow is doing. I am of the school that believes excessive vibrato can defeat its avowed purpose. There are a few top-ranking players who vibrate intensely on every note. But I find it tiring to listen to, no matter how beautiful it may be—something like having cake for breakfast, cake for lunch, cake for dinner, and cake before bedtime. Yet that is their way of playing, and they have their reasons for it, no doubt—or it may be innate. Ysaÿe particularly employed a sound called the *ton blanc*, or "white sound," which is produced with almost no vibrato. Ordinarily if you ask a person whose hand is not well trained to play a passage *senza vibrato*, he will play *senza vibrato* and *senza* almost everything else. There has to be some personality in each note, which is produced by means of sensitivity between the finger and the string. My hand is never absolutely immobile. It is conditioned to the extent that the suppleness and relaxation are never absent.

Lionel Tertis

11

Lionel Tertis and Others

Tertis was an indomitable man. He initiated all this viola business and set the string world on its ear. He was the first person to attempt to persuade the public at large to listen to the viola as a solo instrument and in so doing upset many apple carts. He knew very well that he was not going to get anywhere in his crusade unless he stormed and battered the citadel of apathy that held violists and the instrument in the deepest dungeon of low esteem and regard. And storm and batter he did! It was a heroic battle. For those of us who followed in his train, our task was rendered all the more easy and rewarding because of him. He was the first to insist that the viola was an instrument distinct from other string instruments, that it had a personality of its own. To suggest to him that performance on it was no more than playing the violin a fifth down was to commit the sin of sins and to evoke his swift and devastating wrath. Such a suggestion affects me in the same way.

It is instructive to examine his editions and to observe that here, again for the first time, is a performer who realizes that to finger the viola as one would do the higher-pitched instrument is to do the very thing that brought it into such ill repute. Its tonal recalcitrance is abetted, its sonority muted. It is said that a woman's glory is her hair; the viola's glory is the open strings and the natural harmonics. In this regard it is interesting to examine Louis Bailly's transcription for viola of the Vitali Ciaconna. To finger the viola as the analogue of the violin is indeed a grave error.

During the early part of his career Tertis was reviled—not looked upon as an upstart but a "downstart" (pace G. B. S.). Although a small man he was a feisty warrior and wouldn't take no for an answer at any time from anybody. He had the deepest faith in what he was doing and an unquenchable love for the viola—for what he felt and realized he was capable of. Gradually he forced recognition of the instrument on the concert-going public, particularly in England. Here was something new, to which they *had* to listen. His fight was made even more strenuous by the fact that when he started on his high endeavor there was almost no repertoire for the viola. It has since increased enormously, and this has made it much easier for those of us who have followed in Tertis's footsteps and carried the banner he first held aloft.

He made a perfect pest of himself to composers, more or less sitting on their doorsteps and insisting that they write for him. These days it is somewhat different. Composers will respond to a commission; a nice check fluttering before their eyes usually cajoles them into writing. In Tertis's day, however, that was demonstrably not the case, at least not for him. Consequently the works he was able to wring from reluctant composers are in a way even more important than those we commission today. Most of those who wrote for Tertis were minor British composers—but good ones. Like minor poets, they can be very engaging. He had to convince them that he offered a worthwhile way of communicating their musical thoughts. And, of course, he was convincing.

As to recordings, he had a difficult time persuading companies to let him get anywhere near a recording device. But eventually he recorded a surprisingly large and representative repertory for those early days. When I first started to perform on the viola, Tertis was very generous in his praise. He encouraged me, and as the years went on we became close friends, though I didn't see him as often as I could have wished. At that time his first wife was seriously ill; and as he was an attentive nurse and husband, he led a restricted social life.

164

I don't really owe anything to Tertis so far as my personal style of playing is concerned. While he had some good students, I don't know any violist who, as a player, owes anything to Lionel directly. Lionel had a distinctive and individualistic style, which would have been difficult to imitate—and it would have been foolish to try. He had a unique system of fingering, for example. When first observed, his fingerings in the editions he has published appear bizarre, but they suited him perfectly. And of paramount importance, he was the first man to realize that an artist just does not finger the viola as he does the violin. After he championed the cause of the instrument, those who followed no longer felt ashamed to be playing the viola, despite the fact that some people sneered at him, thought he was mad to attempt solo recitals, and leveled ignoble denunciations against him.

At first Lionel used an uncut Montagana viola. After having played on this large instrument for years, he began to complain of bursitis and kindred ills, which ills he accredited to this rather outsize instrument. Eventually, when he was in his sixties, he decided to retire, and everything seemed to point to the windup of his career. But being a man of considerable resource, he began occupying his time with the designing of a new viola model, one that would give him a sonority after his heart—the sonority he got from his Montagana—but wouldn't produce the physical exhaustion. (Tertis didn't like the viola sound I prefer—the mezzo quality of the Stradivari or Guarneri as opposed to the contralto sound of the Gaspar da Salo and kindred instruments.)

After a great deal of experimenting, he devised a model whose size would be convenient for all viola players and would give the volume and quality of sound he desired. The first man he commissioned to make instruments according to his specifications was Arthur Richardson, a *luthier* of modest reputation at the time. He resided far from London in a little Devon village called Crediton, near Exeter. Tertis also encouraged other English and European *luthiers* to build to his designs and then finally organized a concert at which these new instruments were to be heard. Because of his health at that time, he was unable to participate as he had intended and begged me to take his place. Consequently I was sub-Tertis for that concert.

He was touchingly grateful, and that drew us even closer. As a result of his research we have the so-called Tertis-Richardson viola, which I never actually used, although the viola that William Moennig of Philadelphia made for me incorporated some of Tertis's

165

ideas. At that period too I was using all metal strings, which he also espoused. That his model has not received universal acceptance was, I'm sure, a disappointment to him.

My choice of viola timbre—the mezzo over the contralto—might be surprising to some. But I think the mezzo quality of my Andrea Guarneri is eminently suited for chamber music with Heifetz, for example, because it matches his del Gesù Guarneri violin so well. When I purchased my Guarneri in 1954, Tertis couldn't quite forgive the fact that I had given up using a contemporary instrument. He believed these the only instruments worth playing. Still more to his annoyance, I was using gut instead of metal strings.

My adoption of gut strings came about in the following interesting way. After selling my Amati, which had been cut down—a process which resulted in the emergence of several recalcitrant "wolf" tones and its being too small in volume but never in beauty of sound for some of the halls I was now performing in—I reverted to the Moennig viola and one other that had been made for me by Pierre Vidoudez of Geneva. All this time I had been on the lookout for a fine old Italian instrument. For reasons that are obvious and need no stressing, most violin dealers have a special room in their establishments in which instruments sound superb. I had gone through a series of frustrating and upsetting experiences, being told by dealers that they had a fine Italian instrument—and it indeed sounded wonderful when I played it in the "special room." But when I removed it from the shop and played it under regular conditions, I found it disappointing.

One day in Cleveland in 1954 I received a call from the late Rembert Wurlitzer in New York, who told me that the Lord Harrington viola, my present Andrea Guarneri, which I had known for years by reputation, had just come on the market. This instrument had long been in the collection of a wealthy collector in Chile, and I had been advised that probably it would never be available. I went to New York posthaste, tried it out in the "special room," and of course it had everything I could desire. I thought I wouldn't fool around anymore. If the Lord Harrington wouldn't measure up, I would not bother to look for anything ever again.

That evening I had a concert in the vicinity of New York, close to the residence of Mr. Sacconi, who was the genius—and I use the word advisedly—in Wurlitzer's violin department. I told Wurlitzer that I was going to play the Guarneri that evening, maintaining, "If it stands up to that test, I won't bargain with you. I'll just write out the check for it tomorrow."

166

"Are you out of your mind?" he cried. "To my knowledge, this instrument has never been owned by a professional. I don't think it has been played on for more than a few hours in the last twenty years."

"All the more reason," I returned.

I played my recital and was entranced with the Andrea. The next day I went to Rembert, he named his price, I wrote the check, and the Lord Harrington was mine.

As days passed, however, a sense of dissatisfaction manifested itself—dissatisfaction with the C string. I returned to New York and told Sacconi my troubles. He said he couldn't understand the problem, because the build and proportion of the instrument indicated a good C string. We batted the problem back and forth until I suggested, "Suppose we try a gut A?" Sacconi almost fell upon my neck with joy and delight. People of his tradition are so against the use of metal strings that any indication that an erstwhile sinner has been converted to the truth gladdens the heart. To foist a steel A upon a beautiful, classical Italian instrument was to him much of madness, more of sin.

He put on the gut A string and in a few weeks, like the sleeping beauty, the C string awoke, to a life of new richness. I wouldn't claim that it is a louder C string than one you might find on a fine Gaspar, but the quality is unique. Shortly after that I was recording with Heifetz, who uses both a gut A string and a gut D string on his del Gesù. I thought that I would go all out and use two gut strings on the Guarneri as well. So that's the story of the viola and the strings.

I will now turn for a moment to the composers who wrote significantly for the viola and whose music I performed. Paul Hindemith, himself a violist, figures very prominently among the twentieth-century composers who have left a wealth of music for the instrument. I knew him well and heard him play, but I never discussed his music with him so far as my own performances were concerned. I am greatly stimulated by his music, but I always felt that if he had ever heard me play or heard the recordings I had made of his music (and if he had he observed a lofty disregard), he would have turned thumbs down. I was convinced of a beauty in it that he would not allow in his own performances. He had a horror of anything to do with sentiment—not sentimentality, sentiment. He had that peculiar German outlook *vis-à-vis* sentiment. In the few performances of his that I heard, he appeared to go out of his way,

Primrose in the 1950s

particularly in the beautiful, slow movements, to render the music a little less than engaging.

He had a prodigious left-hand technique, but his bowing I found of questionable grace. He occasionally made it even more so, as in the engaging opening of the second movement of *Der Schwanendreher,* for example, where he ventured to be faintly inelegant so that no one could catch him wearing his heart on his sleeve.

A host of British composers left a considerable store of viola literature. Vaughan Williams I knew, but not very intimately. I don't know whether it was a virtue or not, but I never sought out people. I never chased after engagements either, because I had a horror of being importunate. When I met somebody, I could always tell if that person wished a closer association. If I felt there was any unbendingness, I wouldn't pursue a more intimate association. This is perhaps one of the reasons I didn't know Vaughan Williams better. The only situation in which I was with him for any length of time was during my recording of *Flos Campi*. He was difficult for me to get to know—very shy and withdrawn—but a charmingly noble and delightful man. Hence I but faintly courted his genius, much as I hankered after a work from his pen.

Arnold Bax was among the first English composers to write for the viola, at the behest of Tertis. He was a cricket fan, and we became close friends and played in many village encounters together. He played excellently, as did his brother, Clifford Bax, the playwright. My performances were a hissing and a byword. Arnold, gentle and shy, wrote music of good repute. Few beyond our seagirt isles realize that we had many cultivated and highly trained composers in England.

Elgar and Walton were probably the first ones to gain international approval and acceptance, as more lately did Benjamin Britten. But other composers, such as Bax, Frank Bridge, and Arthur Benjamin, wrote a vast amount of music and were expert craftsmen. I attribute their skill mostly to the guidance they received from Sir Charles Stanford, apparently a very fine teacher who exercised an unyielding red pencil. Stanford was a friend of Brahms, and it was he who brought to my attention the fact that when Brahms writes the word *dolce* he means not only all that it connotes but indicates a slightly slower pace as well. If you examine the Brahms works where this word occurs, you will note that the music lends itself very well to this admonition.

Elgar, as I said, was one of the few English composers to achieve any recognition whatsoever beyond the island. His first acclaim, even before he was accepted at home, arrived with his *Dream of Gerontius* under Hans Richter in Germany. His was, perhaps, the exception that disproved current opinion then prevailing. One can't escape the fact that all the musical nations on the Continent, to say nothing of Russia, looked down their respective noses at English composers and English performers for a long, long time.

169

Primrose in a radio interview in the 1950s

Arthur Benjamin I knew well, and there's a rather interesting story connected with him. One day I saw among his photographic mementos a picture of him in his Royal Air Force tunic from World War I. He was wearing pajamas, his officer's blouse (tunic to English readers), and bedroom slippers and standing in the middle of a field with two other Royal Air Force prisoners and a German officer. Arthur was a gunner and had been called out very early that morning to fight a German squadron. Leaping out of bed, he had only time enough to emplane and take off. His group was to engage the famous Richthofen squadron, but without the baron; he had been killed earlier.

Air warfare during World War I was carried out in a much more

170

chivalrous manner than we have known it to be since, and certain rules and courtesies were observed. One of the unwritten rules required that if a plane was crippled and on its way down it should not be shot at. Benjamin's plane was hit and began to descend, but his foe did not conform to the chivalrous observance. Fortunately he and his crew survived the ensuing crash. The Germans followed them to earth, got out of their plane, and came forward, as they did in those days, to shake hands with their prisoners.

The leader of the German squadron was, of course, at that time Goering—Hermann Goering. I complained to Arthur, "Why didn't you shoot the bastard right then? You would have saved the world an awful lot of trouble!"

Primrose

12

Plight

A national periodical featuring an article on Heifetz attributed the end of the Heifetz-Primrose-Piatigorsky collaboration partly to the hearing difficulty that assailed me some years ago. It was acute enough to cause me concern as a performing artist, but I take solace in knowing that I travel in very good company. Kreisler had exactly the same affliction, as did Beethoven, as so affectingly described in the *Heiligenstadt* letter.

A little medical research reveals that certain ear ailments can be handled by surgery—fenestration, for example. But at that juncture my particular ailment was and is incurable.*

In any case, I should like to divulge some of the origin and history of my plight. When I first went to England after the war, I had a rather severe illness similar to scarlet fever, an illness that often

*According to western otological opinion. An oriental miracle supervened, as I relate in my final chapter, and as Mr. Menuhin has indicated in his foreword.

leaves residual trouble that can affect the ears. I first noticed something amiss about a year later in 1947. I felt the same sensation that one often incurs in high-diving—pressure in the ear, accompanied by an occasional high-pitched noise like that from a steaming kettle. The condition became gradually worse; and although it had no effect on my playing, it was a nuisance. I spoke to my friend Parry Jones, one of the really great Welsh tenors, about my problem. Being typically "clannish," he suggested that I consult the most eminent otologist in London, a Welshman by the name of Ivor Griffith.

The physician examined me, informed my wife of the diagnosis and prognosis, and left it to her to decide whether to break the news that "your husband will either be stone deaf in ten years or in a lunatic asylum." "Why a lunatic asylum?" she asked, and he replied, "The noises will get increasingly worse, and they can become such a torture that the patient may go out of his mind." The noises did become increasingly worse. Two years later my wife finally told me, and I said, "Don't worry. I've learned to live with the noises and really don't notice them unless somehow they are called to my attention." All this time they hadn't had any effect on my actual hearing, so far as music was concerned.

These extraneous sounds are identifiable as pitches. That piercing E in the last movement on the Smetana quartet *Aus meinem Leben*—a high E, E4, which is a little more than three octaves above middle C—is comparable to my particular "tinnitus." That is the same note Smetana had ringing in his head, the note that eventually deranged him. I have it constantly in both ears; it never stops. It has been troublesome, but I just haven't allowed myself to worry about it. Even when it began to interfere with my playing, I still didn't allow it to become a squalid nuisance.

I realized that there are, of course, other things to do in this life—my teaching, for instance. A good friend, an amateur fiddler as well as one of the most renowned specialists in the field of ear medicine, gave me an interesting explanation when I asked, "Why is it that I can hear you accurately in that particular range when you play, but I can't hear myself?" He answered, "You're too close to it. I can't go into technical details because you wouldn't understand them. It's a matter of perspective." Whether or not he was speaking encouraging and soothing words I don't know, but I liked to believe he was correct.

That I can hear accurately at a certain distance is a great misfortune so far as my pupils are concerned, or so they are inclined to believe. Sometimes they think they can fool me, but, alas for them, they can't. I hear all their intonation failings. In short, I have unexceptional "critic's ears." Over the years my hearing problem loomed larger, and I resorted to all manner of tricks to insure intonation in the particular range that was impaired. Then I reached the stage where even the tricks no longer helped. I will say, though, that there has been no deterioration in the last six years that I am aware of.

In addition to the high E that I hear too much of, there is a portion of the scale that I hear too little of, or at least hear inaccurately. The segment that is confused is C3 to A3, two octaves above middle C. I have absolute pitch, but if I hear the notes within that gamut I cannot identify them for certain within a full step, whereas the remainder I hear accurately. The pitches are opaque, something like a picture that is out of focus.

At one point I wore a hearing aid, but it didn't help in the slightest. What I couldn't hear accurately was simply made louder, so I heard it inaccurately louder. There aren't many people who mumble; or, if there are, I just don't admit mumblers into the circle of my intimates. I hear the average person clearly, so my impairment hasn't been too much of a handicap in this respect. It could have been terrible if I had dwelt on it. I am not trying to make myself out to be a hero; I am simply trying to enjoy life and believe something will turn up shortly that will put the whole picture back into focus again.

Since I have had this affliction, I have discovered that there are many people, quite a number being musicians, who are facing what I have gone through but who won't admit it. I suppose it's a case of one sinner always recognizing another sinner. One thing that very strongly affects my condition is the state of my emotional health. If I am emotionally upset, nervous, or depressed, then my ailment is considerably worse. In other words, the blurred quality of my hearing becomes more pronounced and the tinnitus more abusive. But if I'm in normal spirits and in my usual optimistic frame of mind, I can surprise friends, who will remark, "But you're hearing so much better this week than you were last!" My reason for mentioning this is that it might be of help to other people who are having similar problems—many other people, millions of them.

Even if the ear problem hadn't been enough to put an end to my major pursuits, a coronary came close to effacing me from the scene. This was a profoundly interesting experience. I learned that the heart is in some ways well-nigh indestructible. I had a myocardial infarction, which is a long name for the blockage of one of the

Primrose with Franz Rupp at Aspen

vessels leading to the heart. When this happens, the area of the heart adjacent to the artery simply dies, but the heart immediately starts to make new channels for itself. I was one of the lucky ones whose heart made new channels before the whole organ gave up.

So many thousands have undergone the same thing that a description of my sensations is scarcely necessary. However, for those interested, I had warnings two years previously in Portugal, but hadn't associated them with the heart. It was the sort of sensation one gets from swallowing very cold liquid too quickly. It seemed to constrict the esophagus and cause considerable pain in the region of the breastbone. The experience recurred at Aspen, where the altitude is 8,000 feet. The pain receded after a few minutes, but during the night the alarming experience was repeated. I visited the doctor in the morning, certain I had lung cancer, because that was the cause of my first wife's death, and I must confess if I was scared of anything it was that malevolent killer. I was given a thorough examination and nothing could be attributed to lungs or heart.

The medical profession admits that very often the symptoms of cardiac trouble are elusive; and they must have been so in my case, for immediately after I returned from Israel in early 1963, *bang*! It came in the middle of the night. That time I was certain, because the pain was not confined to one place but started drifting over to my left arm. And when it did, I thought: This is it. Strangely enough, however, I wasn't the least bit afraid and was completely confident that I would pull through—so much so that when the ambulance came to take me to the hospital I was highly indignant at having to leave home. I was promptly rushed to the intensive care ward and as promptly went into shock.

Apart from the pain at the onset of the attack at home, I felt nothing—no discomfort. Subsequently I completely lost any thought of myself, as my attention was fully engaged by a little boy near me who was about the age of my own son John. He had brain cancer and kept crying out for his father, who was keeping vigil day and night in the hall outside. When the nurse eventually told me they had taken the child off cobalt treatment and he was going home, I guessed that was the end. I had been so preoccupied with his tragedy day after day and felt so terribly sorry for him that I didn't think of myself. I was only annoyed that I was initially not allowed to shave. I insisted that I shave. I thought, if I'm going to meet my Maker, I'm going to look my best!

My recovery was complete but slow. I had to use walking as therapy, and I've used it sedulously ever since. My walking used to be erratic; at first I was wont to fall down, and just to traverse a block took a lot of effort. The most extraordinary thing, and this may be of interest to string players, was the rapidity with which my playing skills came back to me. I have always had a very strong and supple left hand. I resisted the efforts of early instructors to make me play my technical studies with a completely immobile hand—no vibrato at all. For this reason, I believe, my hand remained lithe even through months of disuse.

177

Primrose relaxing on Springville, Utah, farm

About ten months after the attack I was invited by Heifetz to play chamber music in his home. The summons came on a Wednesday evening and the invitation was for the following Saturday. I started to work on Thursday and within ten minutes I was going without any trouble whatsoever. The bow was a little uncomfortable and it took me slightly longer to get the feeling of balance, but after a half-hour I was in the groove again. It is simply that I had a well-trained and relaxed left hand. The only thing I found disconcerting was that after practicing for a couple of days and then playing the chamber music for several hours on Saturday the tips of the fingers on my left hand were more than a little tender. I believe,

however, that my playing has not been impaired as a result of the coronary.

The reasons for heart attacks are many, so I am told. I have never been a heavy smoker, so in my case little harm can be attributed to nicotine. I believe that one's emotional health is of great relevance. I was deeply disturbed at the time of the onset by various contingencies, and I allowed myself to become overly involved. Since then I have permitted few things to worry me. When a person has been so very close to death, I believe he learns some things instinctively, and one of them—especially if a vital organ is involved—is just to take it easy.

Primrose and Marian Anderson recording the Brahms Songs

13

Legacy

I was fortunate enough to make a goodly number of recordings during my career. Certain of these, the very early recordings with Heifetz, which I have mentioned elsewhere, brought me much satisfaction, as did the recording of the two Brahms songs with Marian Anderson.

Some years ago I recorded Efrem Zimbalist's *Sarasateana*, a fascinating work that demands a high degree of virtuosity. The composer had originally written it for violin and piano, but at my earnest request he transcribed it for viola and piano. I listened to the playbacks, of course, but would not consent to hear it again because I was not satisfied with my performance. However, as my highly critical and musically sophisticated accompanist David Stimer, the producer, and the recording staff were all of a contrary opinion, I grudgingly gave in and surrendered my demand that a lot of it should be rerecorded. But I remained apprehensive. Then a short time ago I heard it again, and I was rather confounded. I think now that it's an extraordinarily good recording. I keep listening for the notes I imagined I had missed or the pianist had missed, but they aren't there—or, more correctly, they are there but are neither missed nor unacceptable. I refused to listen to quite a few of my records for years because of initial dissatisfaction.

I was quite content from the outset with the Bartók concerto, however, and also the *Schwanendreher* and the Walton concerto. I actually made two recordings of the Walton, the first in 1946 on 78 rpm, with Walton conducting, and the second with Sir Malcolm Sargent years later. There is an interesting sidelight to the second recording. The orchestra that was engaged to accompany me was usually enhanced by the presence of the late Dennis Brain, and the concerto contains a number of important horn solos. The day for recording arrived and Dennis, for some reason or other, did not appear. His assistant played, and played very well. When we were listening to the playbacks the following day, Malcolm wished to "pass" the first movement.

"No," I said, "I want to do it again."

"Why?"

"It's a good take," I continued, "but Dennis is here today and I want to have him on this recording." So the horn solos one hears are played by Dennis, an artist so regrettably and needlessly lost to us.

A great deal of my recording was done in the days of the 78-rpm record before the advent of magnetic tape and the LP. We were compelled to put the recording straight onto wax and had to play for some four minutes as accurately as possible. I was always haunted by that awful feeling that I would get to the last five seconds and make a distressing error and have to do the whole thing over again—which reminds me of the occasion of the first recording I made of *Harold in Italy* with Koussevitsky and the Boston Symphony.

The day of recording was preceded by three public performances, two in Boston and one in New York, where all had gone well. We proceeded without hitch until the end of the second movement where, after a few bars' rest, I have to play a harmonic E right at the top of the A string. Prior to this I had never given it any special thought, but during the rest I was suddenly assailed by an apprehension. Supposing I miss this? Here's this quite expensive orchestra costing RCA a lot of money, and all the responsibility is resting on me! It was a hazardous thought, and, as might be expected, I missed the note. We had to start again from the beginning of that particular side.

The second time I didn't miss, but I heard very faintly in the background another E. It was Richard Burgin, the concertmaster, playing just in case I should miss again. It was one of the most gracious and comradely actions I have ever experienced.

This incident reminds me of a story that was told about a student of Klengel, the noted cello teacher. The first movement of the Beethoven quartet, Opus 59, No. 3, contains a tricky passage for cello in ascending broken thirds extending some two octaves. The sufferer plays this alone while the two violinists and the violist wait for him to fling himself to the summit, at which time they rejoin their colleague at his moment of triumph or disaster.

Klengel's student cellist, who was scheduled to perform this quartet, in order to make absolutely certain he could scale the dizzy height, practiced assiduously in private through *four* octaves, reasoning, I suppose, that if he could "go" four octaves, two would surely prove a mere trifle. Came the day, and when he arrived at the infamous passage he couldn't stop. He had to go all four octaves to the top of the instrument, leaving his colleagues dangling in midair.

I tried to approach my recording in much the same spirit as a public performance. In other words, I tried not to sacrifice the emotion of the moment for technical accuracy. I feel a recording should be about as highly charged temperamentally as a performance. I've never resorted to "careful" playing. I always reasoned that if I'm going to miss, I'll miss in the grand manner! Careful playing always sounds just that.

I once heard a recording of a performance that, I was informed, was made up of some hundred splices, and indeed it sounded like it. Heifetz's admirable method of recording calls for a complete performance of a movement entirely without stopping for irregularities. Then he will go through it again and maybe even a third time. If necessary, he will splice an insert from one of the two or three performances, and in that way render the final recording much more alive and spontaneous.

There were other works I would like to have recorded—many concertos, for instance—but that involved the disheartening matter of the orchestras again. The time came when the recording companies were not prepared to record a work with orchestra unless it had been previously performed, or else the entire cost of the orchestra would be the responsibility of the soloist. I am thinking of the Peter Racine Fricker concerto in particular, which was written for me, and which I premiered. It has since been recorded in England.

I regard the Fricker as perhaps the finest viola concerto in the repertoire. When I played it at the Edinburgh Festival in 1953 and later in London, Fricker was comparatively unknown and the English companies weren't especially interested in recording his music. When I brought the work to this country, nobody had heard of him, and of course I wasn't "allowed" to play concertos with the various orchestras. I gave only one performance in this country, at the University of Alabama. The orchestra there was performing a week of English music, and when I was invited to play I suggested the Fricker. It is a magnificent concerto, but I couldn't arouse interest in it.

I have already mentioned Charles O'Connell, of the RCA Victor company, who was a very dear friend of mine, a very brilliant man, and a good musician, and who rendered a significant service to recording in the classical field. His one weakness was that he had an unremitting yearning to conduct. This caused much misunderstanding, as many orchestras would invite him to conduct in the hope of securing a recording contract with RCA and for no other reason. I must honestly say that he was not a good conductor and should have left that aspect of music alone.

His book, *The Other Side of the Record* (New York: A. A. Knopf, 1947), which eventually cost him his job, is a magnificent piece of writing and a trenchant piece of invective. It is an angry book—I read it in manuscript when it was decidedly angrier than the published version. Charles was bitterly, bitterly resentful toward many people in the recording industry, and he fired his broadsides, little caring whom he hit and reckless of their ability to return his fire. He was a very understanding friend who took a great interest in my career and had much to do with my success in recording. Before he severed all connection with the recording industry, I felt a breach in my subsequent relations with RCA Victor, which was to continue until the mid-fifties.

I played and recorded as a soloist, a chamber music player, and an orchestral musician. Of the three, I approached orchestral playing somewhat differently. I think on the whole one has to expend considerably more energy in that role than in the role of violist in a quartet or as a soloist. Conductors especially become riled at the sight of a fiddler using about an eighth of his bow-hair and slouching in his chair. One really had to *give,* and a certain amount of extraneous noise was always produced in the process, which didn't reach the ears of the public either directly or via the microphone. If a performer doesn't play with a certain amount of well-regulated attack in which some roughness is involved, the performance just doesn't get beyond the footlights. A certain amount of rosin must be flying around and, in the case of orchestral playing, the denser the cloud the happier the conductor.

With some good fortune and considerable perseverance, I have been able to enrich viola literature through commissions and my transcriptions. As for those works dedicated to me or commissioned, there is a gratifying number. Often these commissions and dedications gave rise to some interesting situations, one with Benjamin Britten and his *Lachrymae* for viola and piano, for instance.

Britten and Peter Pears were concertizing in the United States in 1949. I met them in New York and we talked about the Aldeburgh Festival, which had been flourishing for several years. Ben, the *fons et origo* of that prestigious event, asked if I would accept an invitation to take part in it the following summer. I said I would be delighted to, but I had no immediate plans to visit "England, home, and beauty."

"If you'll come," he said, "I'll write a piece for you."

"In that case," I promised, "I'll be there."

He promptly composed *Lachrymae*, a series of quite remarkable, highly original, and devilishly ingenious variations based on one of a set of songs of the same name by John Dowland. Ben and I gave the first performance, which of course took place in Aldeburgh, where I also performed the Sixth Brandenburg Concerto with another colleague, Cecil Aronowitz, and with Britten at the continuo. I will never forget *that* performance.

We decided to break out of the dirgelike tempo that is usually afforded that concerto and really give it a spanking, brisk interpretation, especially the first and last movements. Well, we got spanked for it, the public and the press at that period having become inured to the solemn, ponderous, Teutonic tempi fashionable then. But I am still unshakeably convinced that we were right, and I like to believe we broke the pattern. I cannot tolerate Bach being approached as semi-senile. I'm sure that this treatment is the reason the average public has thought of him for so long as a very dull and boring composer—and many still do.

Perhaps the best known of my commissions is the Bartók concerto. In two respects, one of my most rewarding endeavors has been to get composers to write for the viola. Musically the Bartók concerto has had a great success. I have played it more than any other concerto, even the Walton. When I commissioned it, Bartók, incredible though it seems, was an obscure composer. He was known to musicians, but to the great public was "a dismal universal hiss, the sound of public scorn." Aside from performances of the Concerto for Orchestra given by the Boston Symphony Orchestra under Koussevitsky, I don't recall many other performances of Bartók's works.

When I commissioned the concerto, most people, including my manager's office, thought I had made a great mistake. Who on earth was going to ask me to play a concerto by Bela Bartók? I eventually paid his estate what he so modestly asked, and I played the concerto well over a hundred times for fairly respectable fees. So it was almost like getting in on the ground floor when Xerox stock was issued. Hindemith might have been the more logical choice for a commission, and Stravinsky was certainly far better known. But my strong motivation was Bartók's second violin concerto. The Menuhin recording came to my attention and really planted the seed in my mind.

In the case of Hindemith, I knew that he was a difficult man to enlist and probably was influenced by the fact that he had already written four works for viola and orchestra. The Festival Quartet—two of the members were old and close friends of his—solicited a piano quartet from him, something that he had never essayed. But he was not inclined at that time, and shortly afterward he died. Stravinsky I did request, but he turned me down, saying that he was much too occupied with other commissions.

I had known Bartók no more than casually from the mid-twenties. I met him when he visited London during that period and only occasionally after that. I didn't know much of his music, but few did then. In the late spring of 1945 I sought an interview with him in his New York apartment and told him what I was seeking. He was reluctant at first because he felt he didn't know enough about the possibilities of the viola as a solo instrument. I admired his integrity, for at that time he sorely needed money. I asked him not to make an irrevocable decision until he had heard the Walton concerto, which I was playing a couple of weeks later in New York with the late Sir Malcolm Sargent. He planned to come to the concert, which was on a Sunday afternoon, but it so happened that that was a day he felt particularly indisposed and did not attend. He did hear the broadcast, however, and was struck with the concerto and Walton's use of the instrument. He subsequently told me he would definitely accept my commission.

Late that summer I left on a tour of South America and returned with the hope of enjoying the cool of early fall in New England. In

Philadelphia, where I was living at the time, I found a letter from Bartók awaiting me, in which he said that the concerto was finished in draft and "all" that remained to be done was the orchestration, which was routine work (this is reprinted in the preface to the score of the concerto). He wanted to see me, however, to discuss the concerto for reasons that he outlined. It was my intention, therefore, to stop on my way north to see Bartók in New York City. But as it was raining heavily on that day and parking was an insoluble problem, I decided to proceed to my destination and see him on my return.

It was a deplorable decision, one which we all experience when we put off until tomorrow.... On a beautiful day about two weeks later, on my way back from Maine, I stopped outside New York for lunch, picked up the *New York Times,* and read that Bartók had died the preceding day.

If I had been able to consult with Bartók as he proposed, I would have offered a few suggestions that might have altered the concerto in its present form. These suggestions I eventually did make to Tibor Serly, who reconstructed the work from the manuscript left at Bartók's death. One of them, which Serly turned down out of hand, explaining very clearly why he did, concerns measures 102 to 107 in the first movement, where the arpeggios are extremely awkward. I suggested a redisposal of the notes. He felt perfectly certain that Bartók himself would not have accepted the suggestion. It had to do with the relation of the arpeggios that constitute an accompaniment to the solo oboe at that point. Other minor changes were made, but not more than a few measures in all. Of course, in the spirit of performance, I sometimes change a bowing here and there, which I hope doesn't insult the phrasing as the composer intended it. There is a distinct difference between bowing and phrasing, and the distribution of the former for matters of technical convenience must *never* interfere with the composer's intentions in the matter of the latter.

One passage of the concerto is usually misinterpreted, having to do with the matter of the tempos and accelerando of the second theme, first movement, specifically between measures 41 and 52. It is supposed to slow down considerably, and the metronome indication is very wide of the mark. A moment's study will reveal that an accelerando is finalized at measure 52 by a *tempo primo.* There must be some "give" somewhere to prepare that accelerando and a place must be assigned from which it originates. Most performers go straight ahead without respect for the accelerando. Naturally I am influenced by the way I played it and originally understood it should be played.

Curiously, after Bartók's death I heard that the concerto was being rewritten for cello and peddled around. I think the estate was simply looking for a larger commission. At that point, not being in possession of the manuscript, I was withholding payment until delivery was completed. A cellist of some renown was approached but I aborted the scheme, having in my possession the letter from Bartók, which read, in part, "Your concerto is ready in draft."

Halsey Stevens, in his biography of Bartók, offers a less than enthusiastic opinion of the viola concerto as compared with the violin concerto. I do not share his appraisal, but I naturally have a bias in favor of the viola concerto. Peculiarly enough, the concerto was from the beginning a work very accessible to the public ear and certainly among Bartók's more successful works as far as public acclaim, acceptability, and number of performances are concerned.

Serly's part in the reconstruction of the viola concerto is usually a topic of controversy. I saw the manuscript, shortly after Bartók's death, at Mr. Serly's apartment in New York. I was appalled. I didn't see how he could make anything out of it. Fortunately Serly had had experience with Bartók manuscripts, and he knew pretty well what Bartók meant by the sort of musical shorthand he invariably used. I believe that Serly did not add a thing. The manuscript was a type of jigsaw puzzle, and Serly bent over backwards to eliminate anything he was not absolutely certain related to Bartok's intentions. The whole matter was a point that, at the time, I did not feel compelled to raise. I was looking at it from the point of view of a performer, not a researcher. From what I saw, and from what eventually did come out in publication, I would say that Serly didn't add. If anything, he probably subtracted.

I always derived great pleasure from performing the Bartók concerto. I found some difficulty in executing the ending successfully because it arrives so precipitately, and the audience was sometimes a little unsure whether the end had been arrived at. It has to be done in just a certain way, and there has to be a little bit of acting in it, as there should be in all performances. The audience has to know that that is the end—a very exciting end.

I commissioned other concertos by Fricker, Edmund Rubbra, and Milhaud (his second). As previously mentioned, I had my unsuccessful attempts with Stravinsky and Hindemith. I also had quite a number of other composers in mind—Vaughan Williams, for instance. I felt that his Suite for Viola was not really a concerto, or

SEVENTH SUBSCRIPTION PROGRAM

FRIDAY EVENING, DECEMBER 2, 1949, AT 8:30

ANTAL DORATI, *Conductor*

Guest Artist: WILLIAM PRIMROSE, *Violist*

CHORAL-FANTASY, FROM CANTATA NO. 41
    ("JESU, NUN SEI GEPREISET") . . . . . *Bach*

SYMPHONY NO. 96 ("THE MIRACLE"), IN D MAJOR . *Haydn*
    I. Adagio — Allegro
    II. Andante
    III. Menuetto
    IV. Finale: Allegro vivace

CONCERTO FOR VIOLA AND ORCHESTRA . . . *Bartok*
    I. Moderato
    II. Lento — Adagio, religioso
    III. Allegretto — Allegro vivace
        World Premiere

INTERMISSION

PICTURES AT AN EXHIBITION . . . *Moussorgsky-Ravel*

Prelude: Promenade

I. "The Gnome"
    Promenade
II. "The Old Castle"
    Promenade
III. "Garden of the Tuileries"
    Promenade
IV. "Bydlo" (A Polish Wagon)
    Promenade
V. "Ballet of the Unhatched
    Chickens"

    Promenade
VI. "Samuel Goldenberg and
    Schmuyle"
    Promenade
VII. "The Market at Limoges"
VIII. "The Catacombs"
IX. "The Hut of Baba Yaga"
X. "The Bogatyr's Gate at
    Kiev"

(Played without Pause)

The Baldwin is the Official Piano of the Minneapolis Symphony Orchestra

COLUMBIA MASTERWORKS RECORDS—RCA-VICTOR RED SEAL RECORDS

SMOKING. As a courtesy to those attending functions, and out of respect for the character of the building, be it resolved by the Board of Regents that there be printed in the programs of all functions held in the Cyrus Northrop Memorial Auditorium a request that smoking be confined to the outer lobby on the main floor, in the gallery lobbies, and to the lounge rooms.

Symphony Patrons are cordially invited to visit the University Gallery before and after the concert, and during the intermission.

199

Program of the world premiere of Bartók's viola concerto

even a successful work. It was instead a series of short pieces, some of them quite admirable; but others, to me, appeared to be contrived. I was eager to have a concerto, but he wasn't amenable to my suggestion.

I also ardently wished to get a concerto from Sibelius and wrote him to this end, but without success. Roy Harris composed a couple of works that, though not dedicated to me, were more or less intended for me to play with his wife, Johanna. I never did get to the point of asking Aaron Copland directly, but I would have welcomed a work from him with considerable eagerness. Then I was consumed with a desire for a concerto from Prokofiev, but, although Koussevitsky helped me communicate with him, our combined exertions did not elicit a reply of any sort. That was right after the war, when relations between the United States and Soviet Russia were at a low point. Prokofiev died, and I had nothing.

I have sometimes asked myself: If I were concertizing today, would I feel inclined to approach any of the younger composers, perhaps even an avant-gardist, with a commission? I hesitate to answer, because I'm really not sufficiently acquainted with their music. I have students who know more than I do about this aspect of contemporary music; and when they are presented with an avant-garde manuscript, they play it with aplomb, not at all puzzled by what seems to me to be an architect's drawing. I see all sorts of shapes, squiggles, and things that appear significant to them but meaningless to me.

With reference to transcriptions in general, I had a rather amusing encounter with Isaac Stern at a recital he gave at Indiana University when I was a member of the faculty. Isaac programmed the Brahms E-flat sonata, Opus 120, originally written for clarinet and piano but subsequently transcribed by Brahms for viola as well as violin. Who made the violin transcription, I don't know; but I'm secure in my belief that Brahms had little to do with it. I saw Stern before the concert and he apologized for trespassing on my territory. He played the sonata very beautifully, which is what one would expect, and at a reception afterwards I knew he was bursting to know how I had responded.

Purposely, and with mischief aforethought, I refrained from saying anything. Eventually he sidled up to me and put the question directly: "Well, what did you think?"

"Isaac," I replied, "have you seen the TV show, 'Laugh-In'? Do you remember the character who often comes forth with 'very interesting' in a burring teutonic accent? Well, that is my reaction."

Isaac Stern

He laughed and said, "Do you object to it on the violin?"

"Not at all," I said, "but I suspect that more than a handful of clarinet students are waiting outside your hotel door with their knives sharpened!"

Transcriptions of Bach are not infrequently found in a violist's repertory. There are a great many reasons why I prefer the Bach cello suites to the violin sonatas and partitas. One of the main reasons is that, since I have absolute pitch, it disturbs me to hear the Chaconne, for instance, played in G minor when it is originally written in

191

D minor. Secondly, I think very few people are capable of playing the Bach violin works on the viola because of the enormous stretches involved and the chord-playing problems. To be frank, I must say that very few violinists can play these works on the violin. Unless a fiddler has a superb bow technique, he cannot perform these works satisfactorily. And then many of those who do have a fine bow technique still betray a weakness in chord playing. Reaching a compromise is a problem.

When the artist arrives at the chordal passages, he must take great care in performing the chords without rhythmically mutilating the thematic material. On the other hand, if the violinist wishes to keep the thematic material intact and rhythmical, he is apt to produce a scraping, scratching, revolting noise unless he is among the elite I alluded to a moment ago. Tertis started the fashion of playing Bach, and I believe other violists then said to themselves, "Tertis played the Chaconne. Well, let's all play the Chaconne! Let's play all the violin works!"

Where the violin suites are quite unsuitable, the cello suites are much more ingratiating. The chord problems don't obtrude to nearly the same extent, and we violists can play the suites in the same key until we come to the sixth suite, which is usually transposed down a fifth. If we play it higher, in the original key of D major, we get up into the "Northland" and freeze—and freeze the listeners also. I have always held that the viola was more akin to the cello than to the violin anyway.

As for my own transcriptions, I admit that when it comes to composing I haven't an original idea in my head. I tried my hand at it once and the results were deplorable. But I can have a lot of fun with other people's ideas. The Villa-Lobos *Bachianas Brasileiras* No. 5 was an imposing challenge. I don't play the piano and have to be very careful not to write things that are awkward or unplayable. To put eight cello parts into two hands takes some ingenuity. A similar problem occurred in my transcription of the Nocturne and Scherzo from the Borodin quartet. Here, however, as an inestimable advantage, I had the quite active help of Clifford Curzon, with whom I was associated at the time. I made a transcription many years ago, and have since lost the manuscript, of a version for viola and piano of the Hugo Wolf string quartet, the Italian Serenade. I have, since this writing, transcribed it again and wish to put this fact on record in case someone else is fired with the inspiration! My reason, or rather excuse, for transcribing it was the rather prominent part played by a solo viola in the orchestral version.

I am aware, of course, that many musicians condemn transcriptions out of hand. I am also reminded that our greatest transcriber was J. S. Bach. Some critics will go so far as to suggest that the use of transcriptions confirms the paucity of viola repertory. The critics have always been less than fair in this respect. No matter how well a recital might go or how laudatory the review might be, the critics invariably end by saying, "Of course, the lack of literature for the viola is well known." I always thought it grossly unfair, since it must be the critic's duty to inform himself of the existing viola repertory before he makes such a statement. The critic might turn around and say, "Why should I bother with an instrument like the viola?" But I say, "It's your job to bother yourself!"

I have a catalog of viola works that lists, among other categories, over three hundred original works for unaccompanied viola.* The complete catalog comprises 359 pages. Lack of literature, forsooth! I don't claim for a moment that all of these works are masterpieces. But are all works written for piano or violin masterpieces? No, though the percentage is admittedly higher than for the viola. There is, however, plenty to keep the violist occupied, and certainly there is no paucity of literature. The fault of many players is that they limit themselves to a few pieces they know are sure-fire winners. But, with few exceptions, isn't this what most performers do? A good friend of mine, one of the top-ranking violinists, always has to play the Tchaikovsky or Glazounov concertos whenever he is engaged with orchestras of repute. He came to me on one occasion in great excitement, saying that at his next appearance with the New York Philharmonic he was to play the Beethoven concerto, which he plays beautifully. But it didn't work out that way. The Philharmonic boys changed their minds, and he played, as always, Tchaikovsky. He had been typed!

The violinist has a much greater choice of concertos than does the violist, especially contemporary concertos. However, few of them are performed, and we always hear the same works over and over again: the inevitable Bruch G minor, Mendelssohn, Brahms, Beethoven, and a few others. The violist at least has the satisfaction of knowing that almost anything he plays with orchestra has been written in the last fifty years, but is infrequently heard.

In my recitals I have no compunction about using transcriptions, except in Europe. Transcriptions in general are frowned upon there, with few exceptions. In this connection I made a very big mistake

---

*Literatur für Viola by Franz Zeyringer. Verlag Julius Schönwetter, Hartberg, Austria.

on my first appearance in Sweden. I played what would have been an acceptable program here, but they got after me for it. When I returned the following season, I was very careful to choose a program that included no transcriptions—except that, with some trepidation, I included the Brahms E-flat sonata, which they were kind enough to accept.

So far I have given only peripheral consideration to my activities as a teacher. I was not always fascinated by teaching, but I am now. I enjoy it, and, as I commented, I am sorry that some of my colleagues, such as Kreisler, didn't do more of it. They have had vast experience and, in my opinion, should pass it on to the next generation. The first teaching I did of any significance was at the Curtis Institute after I left the NBC Symphony. I had perforce only a small number of students, as the enrollment was deliberately held down and the standards were lofty. It was an all-scholarship school then, and the students had only to pay with their ability. It was the first really close acquaintance with young people I had experienced. I also taught at Juilliard.

There was the short and unfortunately somewhat unfruitful period at the University of Southern California, of which I have already spoken. I also taught during summer months in Toronto, Montreal, Geneva, Banff, Santa Barbara, and Aspen, Colorado, and at the Eastman School of Music. But I'm not in favor of these summer sessions. Eight to ten weeks is too short a time to achieve anything of consequence, and I feel it can't work with any telling effect. I suppose that one can have an influence on a student in a short term of master classes, but to do work of significance requires at least two years or more. I am talking now about the student who is very receptive and already quite well advanced. If one gets a pupil who has suffered from previous bad teaching, one usually can't do anything at all for him in a summer session of a few weeks.

Among students who come to me, I do notice general deficiencies, mainly with the bow. These inadequacies in the right hand can usually be attributed to previous bad training. Parenthetically, it is interesting in this day and age when we have a plethora of Japanese string players to see that they have invariably been exceptionally well trained. Though this may seem quite remarkable, it is really a result of the truly wonderful, but very simple, foundation they receive from Dr. Suzuki and the host of teachers who have been trained by him.

I regard the relationship between teacher and student as a sort of doctor-patient relationship. A doctor has in his file a whole list of

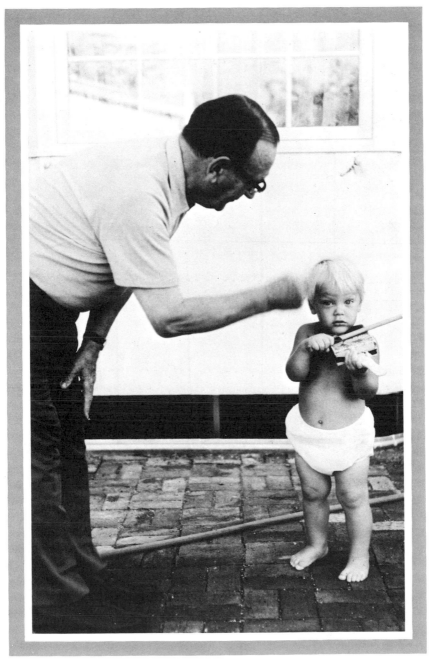

Primrose the pedagogue, with Aaron Dalton

Primrose educating David Dalton on the subleties of the bow

medications to cure certain illnesses according to his skill as a diagnostician. Similarly, I believe I have in my mind a file of different exercises, remedies, and so forth to counteract different bow ailments. When a student comes to study, my problem is to diagnose the trouble and apply the remedy. I must confess that on certain occasions I have been stumped because I find myself too far away from the student's trouble—for instance, the matter of spiccato. I was never taught spiccato. I was told to bounce the bow, and I bounced the bow. I was no genius; it came simply as sheer good luck, and I didn't have to slave at it.

When a student asks me to teach him spiccato, I have a difficult time. I spend much time demonstrating, intending to play long enough so that I may ask, "Do you see what my hand is doing? Do you have the picture in mind?" Then I put him in front of a mirror, tell him to go to work, and leave the room so that he won't be self-conscious. When I come back, I sometimes find that this method has succeeded. Admittedly, it is not a scientific approach, but one day I will learn how to teach spiccato more pedagogically—or perhaps I had better not! Sometimes I call in my assistant, who can then get to the root of the matter better than I can at that moment. Students with such basic inadequacies are not usually those who study viola as a "major" but want to learn how to play for their own amusement and the amazement of their circle of friends.

When a student comes to be taught, I expect him to play an entire work or movement of a work without interruption. I make myself inconspicuous the first time through. I understand that this is how Schnabel taught, and I am probably influenced by the fact that this was the way Toscanini rehearsed. Toscanini would seldom stop. He would go through an entire movement and then go back and take the music to pieces, and the players to pieces also. Sir Adrian Boult once said that to stop a fine orchestra abruptly is like jumping on the brakes of a Rolls Royce. There is nothing more nerve-wracking and exasperating to an orchestra than for the conductor to stop every other bar and point out the obvious: "Now, gentlemen, if you count three and one-half bars before letter B, you will notice that there is a crescendo indicated. At two bars after the same letter kindly take note of the *subito piano,* after which it is marked that we should all make a crescendo to...," and so forth. Such an approach is time-wasting and stupid, and such a conductor earns only the scorn of his musicians. The directions are there in our parts; all the conductor has to do is indicate them with his baton and his gestures.

The obvious benefit that comes from allowing a student to play from beginning to end in a lesson is that he is better able to simulate the actual performance. I think it is a very much more satisfactory way. Ysaÿe used the same approach. And when he offered criticism, he always referred to the admirable aspects before reverting to those which called for censure. Thus he gave the student a feeling of confidence and comfort.

In studying a major work I advise students to practice in a manner similar to that which I used in learning the Bartók concerto when it was first presented to me. Obviously the first thing for me

197

to learn was to solve the technical problems. I applied myself, as I advise my students to do, in the following way, which I believe to be the crux of effective practicing: analyze first and then extract the core of the difficulty. On the second printed page of the viola part, for example, there is a leap from the first position to the upper reaches of the A string. There is absolutely no value in playing a whole bar or so before that leap occurs or in proceeding much beyond it. It is the leap that is the problem, and so I practiced it and repeated it until my arm "memorized" the distance, so to speak, and knew how far it had to travel.

So with the Bartók concerto the first step was to learn the notes, the second to examine the work from a musical standpoint, and the third to memorize. I actually memorized while I was accomplishing the first two stages. After playing the concerto for maybe two years in public, I came close to what I wanted to say in the first place. The best teacher is the public appearance, make no mistake about it.

There are probably no major differences between the students of today and those of my era. I'm not going to be lured into the trap that snares most of us as we increase in years, the trap that leads us to believe that everything that happened fifty years ago was very much better than what is happening today. That is a witless attitude, but very common, I fear. I know that much more is demanded of violists now than when I was a youngster. I shudder what the viola part of *Ein Heldenleben* must have sounded like when it was first played, when the viola of the German orchestras was referred to as the *Penzionsinstrument*. Considering the fact that even in the time of Richard Strauss it was considered slightly immoral to go beyond the third position of the viola, *Heldenleben* must have sounded an appalling hit-or-miss.

Over his years of active public appearances, the artist falls into certain methods of playing and takes the technical aspect of it for granted. When he is suddenly plunged into a teaching situation, where it is mandatory to impart something of importance to a student, which means that he has to verbalize it, then he realizes he has taken these things for granted for so long that it is extremely difficult to dissect and analyze all of it. It is easy enough to pick up the instrument and say, "Do it this way." But that doesn't meet the student's needs in every case. Some are quick to imitate, and that makes life a bed of roses for the teacher. Others cannot, and for them the teacher has to examine his own experience and keep striving to find a way to explain. How to practice economically, for

Primrose in semiretirement

instance, is occasionally not easy to convey to the student, but it is very important, lest all end in exhausted chaos.

I have alluded to the former German conception of the viola and have revealed my bias against their concept of string playing in general. With very few exceptions, and certainly Feuermann was one, I find the German manner of string playing dry and insensitive. It doesn't usually tend toward sweetness of sound, and there's a certain soporific quality about it. Why people like Oistrakh of the Russian school, which is much more akin to the Franco-Belgian style of playing, enjoy such vogue in Germany is puzzling. I don't know of any German violinist who plays in that style. If one must put labels on things (and I rarely approve of this), the Franco-Belgian style is

Primrose the cricketer

certainly much more supple, more ardent, more filled with color, and more effulgent. This also applies to the Russian mode.

Because my first teacher, Ritter, was completely of the German school (he was a pupil of both Joachim and Ševčik), this fact caused some friction between us. It was really very disrespectful of me at that age not to follow his instructions explicitly. I admit again that I'm prejudiced; I know many people who are admirers of German string players. I just don't happen to be one of them.

As an effective diversion from my profession I have nurtured a great interest in and love for sports. I have suggested to my students that they do the same. As I have mentioned earlier, I was introduced to sports in the normal way at school in Glasgow. I naturally was first interested in soccer because Glasgow was the cradle of the game. We played in the streets and alleys; and if we didn't have a regulation soccer ball, we would play with a tennis ball or anything we could get our hands or feet on.

Cricket came later when I lived in London. I suppose the snobbery of the game appealed to me and also the color of it all: the lush green fields and the players in impeccable white flannels. The science of the game fascinated me as well, and as I came to understand it I relished its great skills. I came to know a number of players personally, liked them all very much, and envied them their job. I thought it a marvelous way to earn a living, out all day in the open air and sunshine, traveling all over the world, as the star players did. The more I knew about cricket, the more I appreciated it, just as with American football.

As with sumo later in Japan, when I first encountered football it said nothing to me, but then I determined to make a study of it. As to the inevitable subject of pugilism, some people have the impression that I had an enormous career in boxing, just as some people believe that I played with every important orchestra in the country. Both assumptions are fraught with error. I boxed in school and did a little of the amateur stuff, but was no Cashel Byron. I have intimated that I enjoy chess as a pastime, and it is true that on long journeys my accompanist David and I would while away many an hour at the board.

As a Scotsman, I suppose it is only natural that I have indulged in golf, and I do with no little delight. Had I started at an early age and practiced faithfully, I would have played very well. However, when one, too late in life, embarks on anything that engages and entails coordination, coordination tends to be inconsistent, and for that reason my game is spotty.

Primrose improves his game of chess with international chess master Herman Steiner

There is definitely a relationship between sports and music, particularly between bowing and a golf swing. The stroke one has to use in golf and the action one uses to activate the bow successfully are analogous. Many of the subtle motions that take place in each case are similar. Being an indifferent golfer, I can better sympathize with my students who have trouble with their bowing, since I know that in both one must avoid thinking about the fourteen or fifteen different things that comprise the successful action of the club or the bow. When one can finally forget them and drive without thinking, then one can hit a good ball. The same thing applies to bowing. It's only by constant and correct repetition that these things become second nature and one is "in the groove."

I don't insist that my students cultivate interests outside of music. I only hope that they get the signal. When they come into my studio, for instance, they can see several hundred books on every sort of subject. They know of my interest in football because I'm an ardent fan and attend all the games. I can discuss sumo with my Japanese students with obvious authority, to their manifest astonishment and appreciation. They know of my interest in golf because I'm constantly drawing their attention to the analogy between the golf swing and the bow stroke. I hope that by example and precept this message gets across. It is good to be diversified and not to be steeped only in one subject.

Let us consider some of the artists I have already talked about. Kreisler had a great knowledge of literature in several languages, which was acquired from youth onward over a lifetime, and had more than a passing interest in matters Hippocratic. Victor Babin was not only a highly skilled pianist but an accomplished composer, and his endowment in English was profound. In fact his English prose might be envied by many professional writers. The same thing holds true with Szigeti. I honestly think one will not find among these and other top-ranking musicians any who are devoted to music and music alone.

For my efforts as a musician, my sovereign honored me with the title "Commander of the British Empire." That puts me in doubtful company, however, since the Beatles also belong to the same order, except that I enjoy the great distinction of being a degree higher than they. The Beatles have achieved the "Order of the British Empire." The "Commander of the British Empire" is a cut above that. I mentioned earlier that I had had the doubtful distinction of performing in some rather famous concert halls which soon thereafter burned down. The same thing happened to the British Empire. As soon as I was given this award, it fell apart!

The thing that thrilled me most, I believe, was returning to my apartment in Switzerland, where I was living in 1951, and finding a letter from 10 Downing Street signed by Winston Churchill, informing me that I had been recommended for the Order. It was not till 1953 that I was able to attend an investiture at Buckingham Palace, where the Queen bestowed the honor, a medal with a light blue and pink ribbon, which she placed around my neck. I remember the setting well. While I stood with bowed head before Her Majesty, the string orchestra in the musicians' gallery, which had been discreetly discoursing all afternoon on muted violins, gave forth with "I'm Gonna Wash That Man Right Out of My Hair." I wondered if it was timely.

That I did not attain to a knighthood was no great disappointment, as I knew that I had spent most of my life in America and knew also that, since I was about to become an American citi-

End of a hard day—Primrose and David Dalton

zen, I would be automatically disbarred from the accolade. British conductors of note and directors of the important conservatories, such as the Royal College and the Royal Academy, invariably are awarded a knighthood. The only Americans I am aware of who have been elevated to knighthood are General MacArthur, General Eisenhower, and Admiral Chester Nimitz, to say nothing of Menuhin.

No man could appear more unpretentious than Admiral Nimitz, whom I knew quite well. He looked for all the world like a country schoolmaster and was engagingly modest—the antithesis of MacArthur. He was one of the few war leaders who did not write a book about his experiences, and he had a terrific one in the Battle of Midway, to name but one. In his home he had a trophy room with battle plans, maps, pictures, and all manner of memorabilia. In a certain closet he kept the awards and decorations that he had received from many nations and governments.

There were various orders of knighthood, ranging from Knight Bachelor, for instance, to the most exalted, the K.C.B. or Knight Commander of the Bath. I once asked Nimitz, "Admiral, what is your order?" That was the only time I ever perceived evidence of a small conceit, a touch of vanity. He drew himself up and said, "Why, the Bath, of course." Coming from this simple gentleman, the words left me a little taken aback; but he was at once dignified and charming in the way he informed me.

My career has yielded many rewards. During the time that I was very active, I never thought of branching into anything else. Now that I have had time to reflect and to sort of survey the situation, I realize that I might have been tempted by the medical profession, something that has always interested me, as it appears to interest many musicians, or piloting a plane, among other things, although a jet pilot of some renown once remarked to me that "piloting a plane is a life of considerable boredom, interspersed with some moments of utter horror." In a way I'm rather glad I stuck with the viola.

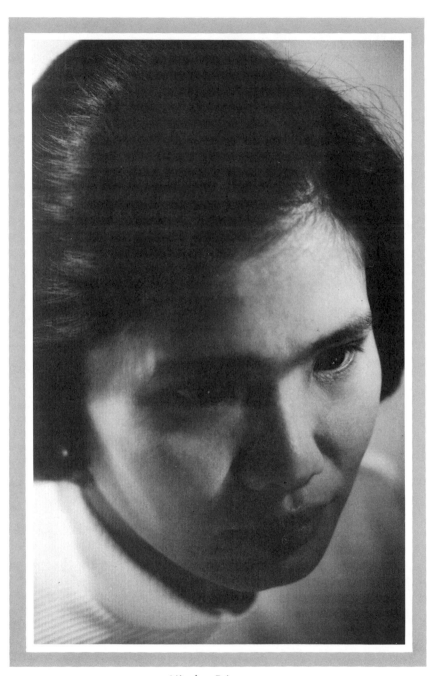

Hiroko Primrose

14

Nippon: Chrysanthemum and Sakura

Some five years have gone by since I wrote the final words of the previous chapter, and I had decided that that was to be the end of it. I had decided that anything I might say about a whole new life that has been vouchsafed me would take up a whole new book, that less would not do it justice. However, as the reader will later perceive, I perhaps do not have sufficient time left. So *little* time. And so I feel impelled to try to compress into these few final pages some of the magic, some of the wonder of this whole new life; and if anyone thinks I am resorting to spruce affectation, three-piled hyperboles, I would beg them to think otherwise, for, indeed, my life in Japan conjured a birth, but not yet a death.

I suppose my love affair with Japan started the moment I set foot on the tarmac at Haneda Airport, but it would be more exact to say that it did when I took to myself a Japanese wife, Hiroko.

The flight across the Pacific in Japan-Air's Jumbo gave me a fore-taste of what I was to experience in the country of Hiroko's birth, while my previous years with her in America had given me, I like to believe, a firm foundation of respect and understanding of the people of her country; this is not easily achieved unless one is so fortunate as I. Westerners have spent years in Japan before coming to grips with the customs of Japan, the language of Japan, the appreciation that is required of the countryside and the teeming cities, the character of the people, and the alveolar that divides the peasant from the city man. I say "alveolar" because it seems to me that "abyss" or "chasm" would be unfitting considering the racial homogeneity. The girl in the rice paddy and the girl on Marunouchi are sisters under the skin. The *Nihonjin* is never anything but that, wherever you meet him.

I liked Haneda Airport (The Field of Wings)—its hustle, its bustle, its confusion. But it was a new hustle, a new bustle, and a curiously different confusion. It is very old as airports go and more than a little decrepit, but it was Japanese and I was indeed as a wondering and bewildered child in a new world where everything is strange but perceived for the first time. Everything is astonishing and ineffable, and one feels that one could not possibly ever become jaded. Indeed, I never was as I "grew up" in Japan.

I liked the breathtaking taxi ride to the heart of Tokyo, and I liked to be disabused of the idea that the Tokyo hackie is an irresponsible madman. He can tell within a couple of inches his propinquity to the vehicle on either side of him for the very good reason that Japanese cars have a rear-view mirror perched on the extremity of each fender (mudguard to English readers), and he never has to take his eyes off the road to discover where his "opponent" may be lurking. Madman though he may appear in a first experience, he is admirably skillful and responsible in his driving, and courteous to a fault. Moreover, he seems to have an endless affair with cleanliness, and when not engaged with a passenger is forever cleaning his vehicle, both outside and inside. He is invariably dressed in black trousers, with a white shirt, a dark-colored tie, and the everpresent white gloves—cotton, to be sure, or similar stuff, but always white.

The drive to the city was through a heavy drizzle and smog and after sundown, though whoever might have seen the sun that day must certainly have been some thousands of feet in the air. It was the rainy season, the fall, but not a season of "mists and mellow fruitfulness." Nevertheless, to my already excited imagination, it gave me strong suggestion of a Hiroshige woodcut, one of the rare monochromes: the vague outlines of the buildings on each side of

208

the expressway, the faint reflections of the multitude of neon signs from the canal (which in the daytime was a noisome pollution of something that no one would call water), and the signs themselves a pendulous penumbra above us. I must confess that as the years went by I was not so romantically disposed toward the season of rains and smog and humidity and heat.

The winter was my season of content, when the strong north winds would disperse the smog and the whole city would coruscate on what seemed to be never-ending days of sunshine. And I could see very clearly Fujiyama (Mt. Fuji, Fuji-san, Mr. Fuji) ninety-five miles away from where I used to board the train at Sugamo station for Ueno. Then there was the brisk walk across the park of that name to Tokyo University of Fine Arts and Music (Geijutsu Daigaku), where I was teaching a small but purposefully very select class of the most engaging and talented pupils it has ever been my lot to encounter. Courteous, neat, well turned out to the best of their respectfulness no matter how much they might be pinched for a Yen.

Always their lessons were prepared to the very height of their several abilities. The little bow on entering my studio, the eager attention throughout the session, the little bow and thank you (*domo arigatō gozaimashita*) on leaving. I was touched by their grace and charm. There was little difficulty with the language. I do not, for an instant, refer to the Japanese language, but the language we used between us. Most of them could speak a little English, and with an adequate dictionary and the fact that musical terms are universal there were few difficulties in this respect.

The language itself? Heaven protect me! It is reported that, after long and fruitless efforts to master the tongue of the "heathen," St. Francis Xavier reported to his Jesuit Order in Europe that it must have been devised by Satan to prevent the teaching of Christianity to the natives of Nihon. I have been told on good authority by a reliable American acquaintance that it takes fifteen years of study and living in the country, absorbing the mores and customs of the people, to become a really adequate master of the Japanese language. I believe him. Fortunately, having a Japanese wife, whose English is fluent, I did not have to suffer the frustration of the language barrier and even got to the point of uttering a few phrases on my own. I was just above the category of the bemused American *gaijin* (foreign) traveler who with a sudden brainwave thought to avail himself of a suggestive form of mnemonics to assist him in saying at least "good morning" (*ohio*) and "thank you" (*arigatō*). *Ohio* was simple enough and *arigatō* seemed to suggest alligator. In its appropriate place *ohio* came out all right, but his recall betrayed his mnemonic at a crucial moment and "thank you" emerged as "crocodilo." I did manage to learn most of the Katakana and Hiragana syllabaries that afford the language its prepositions, conjunctions, cases, and other parts of speech—and are used in the matter of foreign words and scattered among the Kanji—of which there are only some two thousand one has to learn, like pepper from a pepper mill. But that is as far as I ever got, and I was more than a little proud of this accomplishment.

To get horribly and frighteningly lost, as I once did in Tokyo, and to be without the language can be a dismaying experience. Tokyo is an agglomeration of towns, each *ku* or *cho* being a city unto itself, and apart from the great main boulevards one encounters a maze of tiny, twisting streets with their everlasting delights of tiny shops, most of them open-fronted and adorned with all sorts of tasteful and colorful decorations: little banners, imitation flowers in every shape and shade, streamers and ribbons, lanterns and lights—but definitely not the place for the illiterate *gaijin* to get lost! Few of the streets are named, even if one could read the signs, and taxis are infrequent, even if one could make the driver understand where he wished to go. Usually, if the sun was visible and I knew which was west, east, north, or south, I had little difficulty in finding my way back to the main artery of my *ku*—Bunkyo-ku. And in downtown Tokyo the two tallest edifices in the center were the Kasumigaseki Building and Tokyo Tower. They were the marks to guide my wanderings.

One dismal day it befell that I was wandering in the mazes of Bunkyo-ku, delighting in all the sights, sounds, and perchance effluvia, when I realized that I had not the slightest idea where I was and had no sun or any other sign to instruct which way to turn. For a moment I gave little thought and but a light laugh to the grim situation, but I soon realized that I really was in a fix of monumental proportions. I have always been one of those annoying people who count everything: I count all the steps in a stairway, I count all the lamp posts in a neighborhood street, and so on. I need not labor my weakness. I had counted the placing of the bright green pantographs on the cars of the Yamanote Line which traversed Bunkyo-ku in part and embraced central Tokyo in full. It was the line I used to get from Sugamo to Ueno, as I mentioned a while back. On the even-numbered cars I was without any doubt that the train was proceeding in the direction of Tokyo station, on the uneven numbers in the direction of Shinjuku. That seeming bit of idle knowl-

210

edge saved me. I observed a train pass over a railway arch in the street which I was then pacing in no little panic. It was Tokyo bound. I turned in that direction, kept the railroad embankment always in sight, and reached my main street, Hakusan-dori, and the safety of my flat with grateful appreciation of a tiresome habit.

I could go on at great length about all the charms, delights, and happinesses of Tokyo, Nagoya, Kyoto, Matsumoto, the Isu Peninsula, and so forth, but I have to reach the end of this book in some sort of reasonable time. So, I very much wish to wind up (but again at some length, I must warn the reader) with an account of my encounter with two of the most phenomenal men in all my wanderings in my favorite country (and I met many striking characters): Dr. Haruchika Noguchi and Dr. Shinichi Suzuki. I had heard of Dr. Noguchi before I set foot in Japan, and I would go so far as to say that he is known throughout the reaches of the Islands. Philosopher, poet, thinker, scholar, scientist, the Seven Sages in one human, and dominantly and paramountly a healer. A quack? Well, I suppose by western observance, perhaps. By Oriental standards, NO! Nothing of the medicaster, nothing of the Pharisees and hypocrites, but all of humanity! Delicately skeletoned and wee as so many of the Japanese are, his ageless spirit pervaded the farthest corners of his clinic in Setagaya-ku, which was reached by a tangle of changes and interchanges in the incredible web of subways and overhead railroads in and around Tokyo. Thank heavens I had learned enough of the Hiragana and Katakana to decipher the names of the sundry stations where those changes and interchanges should be made. Of course, Hiroko, my wife, had accompanied me on my first pilgrimage and that, plus a good memory, helped no little.

It would be idle to attempt to describe the clinic, its *ambiente* at this moment. A whole book could be devoted to it, and indeed whole books have in Nihongo (I must show off my expertise in the language!), but, so far as I know, no translations are at hand. The same conditions will prevail when I come to discuss Suzuki and Matsumoto.

I wrote much earlier—years earlier—that I would reserve my observations and experiences of and in Japan to a book I had in mind for later publication, but, as I have indicated at the beginning of this chapter, time is pressing. Why it is pressing will be revealed in due course, and the indulgent reader will clearly understand.

Dr. Noguchi, to whom I had been introduced by Dr. Suzuki, knew about me, had many of my recordings, and knew about my deafness problem. Ill tidings travel apace. He promptly invited me

PHOTO BY HIROSHI FURUSE

Dr. Noguchi, Primrose's physician

to attend his clinic, and indeed I did without further hesitation. Months passed under his loving care, and little by little that section of the scale that had proved treacherous succumbed to his compassionate ministrations. To be sure, my acuity to the spoken word took longer. But who was I to care too much about the drivel of vocalizings that engulf us, especially as I could not understand the language of the country in which I was living? Dr. Noguchi, who commanded very handsome fees, insisted on treating me for nothing, such was his deep regard for music and musicians. Let the cynic, if he will, exclaim that the two statements are mutually exclusive. The cynic isn't deaf, and if he is, he is not compassionate. Dr. Noguchi did not devote himself only to people in my condition. He gentled and succored many with ailments far removed from mine, and to my knowledge many other musicians were the beneficiaries of his generosity because of his great love of music.

My first experience of a visit to his clinic in Setagaya-ku was a very moving and revealing experience, as was each succeeding one. There was, of course, the ceremony of removing one's outdoor footwear in the entrance and putting on the *zori* (heelless slippers) supplied to all guests in Japanese homes and many offices too. These in turn are dispensed with when one enters a room with *tatami*, the mats made of rice straw and all of uniform size, found in any sort of ceremonial room. It is interesting, in this connection, that the size of a room is referred to not in numbers of square feet but in the numbers of these mats it can accommodate. Stocking feet, or *tabi* if one has them, arc *dc rigueur*. The waiting patients sat around in comfortable easy chairs reading or meditating and contemplating the Japanese garden. Others, in a portion of the very large room that was raised above the general level, would be practicing the various yogalike exercises that were deemed necessary to his or her form of treatment. The novitiate was always carefully and attentively instructed in these by the doctor's assistants. The time of waiting over, the patient would join a few others who were seated cross-legged, as is the Japanese custom (and one that caused me considerable discomfort in the beginning), hands folded in the lap, in the doctor's treatment room. The doctor, clad in the traditional male *haori akama*, would attend each patient in turn; and the patient, on leaving as on entering his presence, would offer an obeisance along with the customary *domo arigatō gozaimashita*, acknowledged by the doctor's murmured thanks in turn. Everything was a murmur in the clinic; a hush pervaded, and the only other sound of which one was conscious was that of quietly played chamber music relayed throughout from a central record room. It would be almost idle to stress the therapeutic value of that additional attention. I eagerly looked forward to these weekly visits, which continued so long as I lived in Japan, to say nothing of his monthly chamber music evenings performed by many of his grateful patients and followed by the ages-old tea ceremony. His death was mourned by a host in Japan and by many abroad who had had the inestimable benefit of his gracious care.

I mentioned earlier that I was introduced to Dr. Noguchi by that other wise and impressive friend, Shinichi Suzuki. My first meeting with him, when my wife Hiroko and I made the pilgrimage to Matsumoto, the headquarters and the *fons et origo* of all his philosophy and teaching, was accompanied by a very considerable amount of skepticism. All my defenses were up, all the decks cleared, all my critical guns primed. I could not accept what I believed to be an "assembly line" approach to teaching the violin. Like many of my professional colleagues, particularly in America, I darkly doubted the efficacy of the "Suzuki Method," but, like most of the others, without understanding a single one of his motivations and aspirations. I had heard some of the Japanese children perform in a concert given by a group that was then touring the world.* I could not help being impressed. Their little bow arms were a model, their intonation was beyond criticism, the sounds they produced were alluring, their rhythm was impeccable, and their musical sensitivity was irresistible, but I explained all that away with no little cynicism and self-satisfaction. Of course they were a very carefully chosen group, but I was told they couldn't read music, were not creative, and learned everything by rote—probably from recordings, I guessed—and so, with a whole roster of objections, I refused to accept anything as being other than part of a huge hoax.

Again, I had many who flattered my scorn by scorning in the same way. A specially chosen group? Of course. And I had heard not a few American youngsters, home produced, who played

---

*Shinichi Suzuki wrote in connection with this tour in 1970: "I consider it a great honor to have been invited by many progressive universities and other institutions to take part in demonstrating a method by which the great potential inherent in all children can be developed.

"Twenty years ago it would have been inconceivable that a group of over 1,000 children, ages five to thirteen, would be playing the Vivaldi Concerto or the Bach Double Concerto on their violins.

"After the war, when the remains of many destroyed buildings were seen all over Japan, I started this Movement, realizing how these innocent children were suffering from the dreadful mistake made by adults. These precious children had no part in the war, yet they were suffering most, not only in lack of proper food, clothing, and homes, but more important, in education.

"Teaching music before the war, I found to my amazement that small children develop their abilities far beyond what anyone would expect of them. Given normal mental ability, any child can be taught to appreciate music.

"The children here today are testimonials of my thirty years' study. We are not teaching them to become professional musicians.

"I believe that sensitivity and love for music and art are more important to people of all ages. These are the things that enrich our lives. I urge you to explore this new path for the education of youngsters so that *all* children will enjoy the happiness they deserve."

Dr. Shinichi Suzuki

abominably, and I was convinced that I would hear many more in Japan. I learned considerably later that a host of Suzuki quacks and gammoners practiced their fourflushing in the United States (and elsewhere, to be sure). It is easy enough to buy a few of his books for a small outlay and "set up shop." The mothers are gullible and do not know that they are being "conned." Moreover, it keeps the children occupied and off the street corners, and the charges are not exorbitant. That is very fine up to a point, but heaven forbid that these activities should disport themselves under the banner of the so-called "Suzuki Method."

I write "so-called" because "Suzuki Method" is an appellation frowned upon by Suzuki himself. Well, hardly frowned upon. His philosophy does not admit frowning on anything. I think that is the quality that engages him so patently to young children. Patience, tolerance, and love are his beguilings, and that is why he gives to the lives of these infants an ineffable joy. It is not his purpose to turn out assembly-line prodigies; it is, rather, to enrich their young lives and make them lovelier human beings. Those of his charges who have shown an implacable desire to adopt the profession of violin playing as a career he has turned over to the most highly regarded professional teachers. He insists that he is not a professional in this line and frequently refers to himself as an amateur.

My earliest impression from my first visit to the Talent Institute in Matsumoto was the pervading feeling of happiness, joyance, and beatitude. If he has done nothing else he has, unwittingly perchance, helped solve the problem of the generation gap. The devoted parents (and how very devoted are Japanese parents, especially the mothers) bring their infants in arms to the Talent Institute to be exposed to music, to be weaned almost on beautiful sonorities, to say nothing of observing the motions of the older sisters and brothers. And how important that is! I have related much earlier in this book how I sat in my father's parlor and with two pieces of wood ran through all the muscular activities of violin playing. Children are nothing if not counterfeiters, simulators. But here, I suspect, I have painted myself into a corner. I was, after all, being groomed by my aspiring father for a professional career, and I have at the same time been insisting that Suzuki has no observance of professionalism. After all, don't his young charges play piano in a most engaging fashion, cello for that matter, the Koto, beguiling *instrument ancien* of Nippon, learn the ancientness of cursive *Kanji* and the recitation of endless *Haiku*? What better way to raise a child? Has that anything to do with professionalism? Has that any-

216

thing to do with his complainers? Has that anything to do with his ability to make these youngsters adjusted and well tempered in a magic country that was first befouled by the evil of man's inhumanity in Hiroshima and Nagasaki?

To return to my earlier criticisms: I have already admitted that I almost succumbed to the blandishments of the charming Japanese children then on a world tour, but I had been able to resist with the passing thought that they were a specially chosen group. It is my unhappy observation that when we are determined to denigrate that which does not meet with our approval we allow our intelligence to desert us. Why should the Talent Institute put on display anything but its best wares? Would any other organization? They can't read music, I was told. How monstrous! But, as Suzuki cogently questions, how many of us would have our children remain speechless until they were able to read their primer? That they are not creative is, I am persuaded, perhaps the most unintelligent observation of them all. What instrumental performer is creative? Re-creative, to be sure, and some to an extent that borders on creation. But creative, never. They learn by rote, probably through the medium of recordings? How shabby, how contemptible. But do any of us develop without a model? What are teachers for? Yes, to teach us to bow and to develop the fingers of the left hand, or both hands in the case of pianists, but the best of them to inculcate an awareness of musicality, of traditional musical values from which, according to our sundry gifts, we may take wing. But a model we *must* have, and an instructor we must have. I am unaware that Mozart went without strict and disciplined schooling. All these frangible sticks to beat that dog Suzuki! All these animadversions, all that carping and caviling inspired by envy and animus and, as is usually the case, without the least understanding of what it is all about. Not the mass production of fiddlers but the enrichment of little lives, to say nothing of the integrated personalities that emerge from the experience.

How many of us can claim to have done as much for our own students? I would at this point admonish the ambitious mother (with whom one usually associates the child in Suzuki training) to eschew ambition unless, of course, she is bent on her baby becoming another Heifetz, a most unlikely happenstance. Not every mother is likely to have a Hiroko Primrose at hand in the neighborhood. Let me hasten to point out that I do not intend to insist that my wife is unique. Indeed, she is not—in Japan. There are many, both men and women, nurtured by Suzuki and guided by many years of direct association, who are eligible to call themselves practitioners of the Mother Tongue Method. (Suzuki prefers that appellation to "Suzuki Method," a phrase originating from his American disciples.) The mother and child are unlikely to be able to take off for Japan and a sojourn in Matsumoto. But let her beware the false prophet who avails himself of a few of the source books—or all of them, for that matter—hangs out his shingle, and sets himself up as a "Suzuki Method" instructor.

I do not wish to suggest that these *unaccredited* teachers are all fraudulent. By no means. Only some of them. The others are, no doubt, excellent teachers of the violin for beginners. But in all honesty they must sail under their own colors. To engage the magic and drawing power of the Suzuki name is greatly tempting, but to yield to the temptation is rather shabby in my judgment. Suzuki's method of teaching violin is, *per se*, not very much different from many others. But, as I keep on insisting, he is not a professional violin teacher, as *he* often insists too. His uniqueness lies in his impressive ability to develop these little ones and to enrich their lives. And his disciples can perceive this only by constant association with him, absorbing his philosophy and his psychology, and those, like Hiroko Primrose, are bound to be much closer to all this in that they are Japanese and are ethnically involved. No westerner, in my opinion, can ever completely achieve this, even those like William Starr and a few others who have spent much time in the *ambiente* of Suzuki and Matsumoto. To purchase his books and "set up shop" is a discreditable come-on, to be censured with no little scorn. Starr would heartily agree. And the common three-month pilgrimage has not a great deal to commend it, but it is better than nothing.*

I am constrained to believe that a visit to Matsumoto and association with Dr. Suzuki of at least three months is mandatory before anyone can claim to be a qualified exponent of the Mother Tongue Method, and even that is all too short. There is in America, however, the happy contingency that one may avail himself or herself of association with a William Starr or a John Kendall, both of which knowledgeable fellows have frequently refreshed their knowledge at the *Urquell*, the Fountainhead, and have written with authority and cogency on the whole subject. To my mind, and it must be obvious at this juncture, there is no doubt that association with a native

---

*It is interesting to note that Mrs. Lois Shepheard of Melbourne, a leading Australian exponent of Suzuki's teaching in that country, embellished her frequent visits to Matsumoto by learning Japanese in order to understand more deeply his writings and his thinking.

teacher, close historically, philosophically, philologically, spiritually, and in intelligence and compassion, is greatly desirable. However, it is not always convenient or in a fair way of attainment. In countries other than Japan there are, to be sure, competent and adequate choices, but I stress careful choice, careful investigation, and—well, *caveat emptor*. Further advice is unnecessary.

Elsewhere in this final chapter I have hinted that I am aware that time is pressing and that I had better get down now to what may prove to be my valediction before it is too late. The following words might, therefore, belong to the chapter entitled "Plight," for, indeed, I am in a plight. Those fellow sufferers who have glanced at this manuscript while it was lying fallow over the past five years, those who have suffered ear difficulties and coronaries, have been good enough to tell me that what I have written on these matters has given them courage and renewed hope. I, in turn, have received courage, if not quite renewed hope, from this knowledge. I have always felt objective and impersonal in moments of crisis, as I related before in the moment that everything went "agley," as we Scots are wont to say, during a performance of the Bartók concerto with a famous conductor and his distinguished orchestra. I felt thus about my massive heart attack. I felt the same way about my impending deafness when my first wife informed me of Dr. Griffith's diagnosis and no less his prognosis. (British readers, if any, will forgive me. As he is a Harley Street specialist I should more properly refer to him as Mr. Griffith.) I must assure all who have traveled with me thus far that I had exactly the same detached response when, shortly before I undertook to write these parting words in this book, I came face to face with an inoperable cancer. My immediate reaction was that we are all of us under sentence of death from the moment we are born. We are the only living creatures (so far as we know) aware of this fact, we must come to terms with it, and if it is not one thing it is another. Cancer always invokes a sense of something grim, implacable, and sinister. But aren't all the disorders that terminate our lives of the same character? My first wife died of cancer, and when she called me from our flat in Switzerland (I was in London) to inform me of the unbelievable verdict I was assailed by an emotion many times more bleak and shocking than I am aware of at this moment—something like being winded at football. My breath would never, never return. I am convinced that the good friends, the relatives, and the loved ones are those who experience the despair and hopelessness. Malcolm Muggeridge, in his book *Jesus Rediscovered*, maintains that he never felt a true relationship with this

world, was never an indivisible part of it, but rather that he was here only for a brief sojourn—anyway, words to that effect. He longed with an exquisite ardor for the world to come. I must confess I do not feel this way about the present life. I love this world and all that is good in it and of good report. At the risk of being regarded as maudlin I am bound to say that I deeply respond to the awe-inspiring-ness of great vistas, the restfulness of an English village, the glory of music and pictures and poetry and gracious prose, the thankfulness of recalling Richard Crooks singing *Du bist die Ruh,*

the soft supplication of a sunset, and the fury of storms at sea as when I exulted in a North Atlantic gale. Someone once wrote: "It's been a lovely party, I really hate to leave it. It's been a lovely party, I really must repeat it."

It *has* been a lovely party, and while I don't altogether agree with Muggeridge about his detachment from this world, I do agree with him about the glories of the world to come. "Port after stormy seas, . . . death after life does greatly please." So, until the curtain drops: *Ave atque vale!*

Discography

Compiled from *L'Alto et ses interprètes,* by Dr. François de Beaumont.

AGUIRRE, Juan B. (1868–1924)

Huella, for Orchestra
Arrangement for viola and piano
  W. Primrose, viola / D. Stimer, piano
  45 rpm—Victor 49-0918
  78 rpm—Victor Vic. 12-1109

BACH, Carl Philipp Emanuel (1714–88)
Solfeggio for Clavier in C Minor, "Spring's Awakening" (W 117/2)
Arrangement for viola and piano
  W. Primrose, viola / J. Kahn, piano
  45 rpm—Camden CAE 244
  78 rpm—Victor Vic. 10-1098

BACH, Johann Sebastian (1685–1750)
Komm süsser Tod, for Voice (No. 42, Schemelli)

Arrangement for viola and organ (or piano)
W. Primrose, viola / V. de Tar, organ
American Columbia AmC AAL 33
78 rpm—Victor Vic. 11-9117/Vic. 16316
(Reedition 1946) in VM 675

Suite No. 3 for Orchestra: Air
Arrangement for viola and piano
W. Primrose, viola / D. Stimer, piano
45 rpm—Victor 49-0918
78 rpm—Victor Vic. 12-1109

BACH, Wilhelm Friedemann (1710-84)
Sonata for Viola and Piano in C minor
Arrangement (Pessl)
W. Primrose, viola / Y. Pessl, piano
78 rpm—Victor Vic. 18107/8 set M 807

BARTÓK, Béla (1881-1945)
Concerto for Viola and Orchestra (posth. T. Serly)
New Symphony Orchestra / Serly / W. Primrose, viola
Bartok BRS 309 / World Record Club CM 20

BAX, Arnold Edward Trevor (1883-1953)
Sonata for Viola and Piano in G Major (1921)
W. Primrose, viola / H. Cohen, piano
78 rpm—Eng. Mus. Soc. Vol. II / American
Columbia AmC. 11151/4 D set M 386

BEETHOVEN, Ludwig van (1770-1827)
Duo for Viola and Cello in E-flat Major (mit zwei obligaten Augengläsern) (1795)
W. Primrose, viola / E. Feuermann, cello
RCA Victor Vic. 1476
78 rpm—His Master's Voice G. DB 6225 / Victor Vic. 11-8620

Notturno for Viola and Piano, Opus 42 (1804)
Arrangement by the composer from the Serenade in D Major, Opus 8, for Violin, Viola and Cello (1796)
W. Primrose, viola / D. Stimer, piano
78 rpm—Victor Vic. 12-1043/5 set DM 1336

BENJAMIN, Arthur (1893-1960)
Cookie, from San Domingo
Arrangement for viola and piano (Primrose)

W. Primrose, viola / V. Sokoloff, piano
78 rpm—Victor Vic. 11-8947

Elegy, Waltz and Toccata, for Viola and Piano
W. Primrose, viola / V. Sokoloff, piano
78 rpm—Victor Vic. 11-9210 / 1 set M 1061

Jamaican Rumba (No. 2 of Two Jamaican Pieces), for Orchestra (1940)
Arrangement for viola and piano (Primrose)
W. Primrose, viola / V. Sokoloff, piano
78 rpm—Victor Vic. 11-8947

Matty Rag (No. 1 of Two Jamaican Pieces), for Orchestra (1940)
Arrangement for viola and piano (Primrose)
W. Primrose, viola / V. Sokoloff, piano
78 rpm—Victor Vic. 11-8947

Romantic Fantasy, for Violin, Viola and Orchestra (1935)
RCA Victor Orchestra / Solomon / J. Heifetz, violin / W. Primrose, viola
RCA Victor Vic. LM 2149 / LSC 2767

BERLIOZ, Hector (1803-69)

Harold in Italy, Op. 16
Boston Symphony Orchestra / Koussevitzky / W. Primrose, viola
RCA Victor Vic. LVT 1013 / LCT 1146

Boston Symphony Orchestra / Munch / W. Primrose, viola
RCA Victor Vic. LM 2228 / RB 16084 / SB 2016 / 630336(?)

Royal Philharmonic Orchestra / Beecham / W. Primrose, viola
Fontana KFR 4002 / Columbia Col. ML 4542 / C. QCX 10005 / FCX 178 / C CX1019 / Philips G 03627 L

Boston Symphony Orchestra / Koussevitzky / W. Primrose, viola
78 rpm—His Master's Voice G. DB 6261/5 / Victor Vic. 11-8751/5 set M 989

BLOCH, Ernest (1880-1959)

Five Pieces for Viola and Piano: 1. Rhapsodie Hébraïque, 2. Meditation,   3. Processional 1,   4. Processional 2,   5. Processional 3 (Affirmation). [1, 4, 5 = Suite Hébraïque]
W. Primrose, alto / D Stimer, piano (1-5)
Capital P 8355

Suite for Viola and Piano in A Minor (1918-19)
W. Primrose, viola / D. Stimer, piano
Capitol P 8355

W. Primrose, viola / F. Kitzinger, piano
78 rpm—His Master's Voice G. DB 3977/80 / Victor Vic. 15475/8
set M 575

BOCCHERINI, Luigi (1742-1805)
Sonata for Cello and Continuo No. 6 in A Major
Arrangement for viola and piano (Primrose)
   W. Primrose, viola / J. Kahn, piano
   Japanese Victor JpV. SD 3090
   78 rpm—His Master's Voice G. ED 220 / Victor Vic. 17513

BRAHMS, Johannes (1883-97)
Chorale Preludes for Organ, Opus 122, No. 10, "Herzlich tut mich verlangen"
Arrangement for viola and organ (de Tar)
   W. Primrose, viola / V. de Tar, organ
   American Columbia AmC. AL 33
Lieder for Contralto, Viola and Piano, Opus 91
1. Gestillte Sehnsucht,   2. Geistliches Wiegenlied   (1884)
   M. Anderson, contralto / W. Primrose, viola / F. Rupp, piano
   78 rpm—Victor Vic. 18507/8 set M 882 / His Master's Voice G. ED
   352 (2)
Sonata for Viola (or Clarinet) and Piano No. 1 in F Minor, Opus 120
   W. Primrose, viola / R. Firkusny, piano
   Capitol P 8478/K80336 / Seraphim sera. 60011
   W. Primrose, alto / W. Kapell, piano
   78 rpm—His Master's Voice G. DB 6953/5 / DB 9247/9 / Victor
   Vic. 11-9487/9 set M 1106
Sonata for Viola (or Clarinet) and Piano No. 2 in E-flat Major, Opus 120
   W. Primrose, viola / R. Firkusny, piano
   Capitol P 8478/K 80336 / Seraphim Sera. 60011
   W. Primrose, alto / G. Moore, piano
   78 rpm—His Master's Voice G. DB 3314/6 / Victor Vic. 14736/8
   set M 422

CHOPIN, Frédéric (1810-49)
Nocturne No. 2 for Piano in E-flat Major, Opus 9, No. 2
Arrangement for violin and piano
   W. Primrose, violin
   78 rpm—Columbia C. 9258

DVOŘÁK, Antonin (1841-1904)

Gypsy Songs, Opus 55, No. 4
Arrangement for viola and piano, for viola and orchestra
  W. Primrose, viola / F. Rupp, piano
  78 rpm—Victor Vic. 8730

Humoresque for Piano, Opus 101, No. 7 in G-flat Major
Arrangement for viola and piano, for viola and orchestra (E. de Luca)
  W. Primrose, viola
  45 rpm—Camden Cam. CAE 251
  Victor Symphony Orchestra / O'Connell / W. Primrose, viola
  78 rpm—Victor Vic. 18222

Symphony No. 5 (9), 2d movement
Arrangement for viola and piano
  W. Primrose, viola / F. Rupp, piano
  78 rpm—Victor Vic. 11-8730

HANDEL, George Frideric (1685-1759)

Concerto for Viola and Orchestra in B Minor
(Realization by Henri Casadesus)
  Victor Sym. / Weissmann / W. Primrose, viola
  Camden CAL 262

  Chamber Orchestra / Goehr / W. Primrose, alto
  78 rpm—Columbia C. LX 605/7 / LWX 189/91 / GQX 11023/5 /
  American Columbia AmC. 68975/7 D set M 295

Victor Sym. / Weissmann / W. Primrose, alto
  78 rpm—Victor Vic. 11-9612, set M 1131

Sonata No. 3 in A Major, Opus 1 (Sonata for Violin No. 1)
Arrangement for viola and piano
  W. Primrose, viola / J. Kahn, piano
  78 rpm—Victor Vic. 17478

Sonata No. 9 in E Major, Opus 2, "Trio" (Sonata for 2 Violins and Continuo)
Arrangement for violin, viola, and piano
  A. Spalding, violin / W. Primrose, viola / A. Benoist, piano
  (*Adagio*)
  78 rpm—Victor Vic. 18241 in M. 838

Suite No. 7 for Clavier in G Minor, Passacaglia
Arrangement for violin and viola (Halvorsen)
  J. Heifetz, violin / W. Primrose, viola
  RCA Victor Vic. LVT 1014/LCT 1150

J. Heifetz, violin / W. Primrose, viola
78 rpm—Victor Vic. 11-8151 / His Master's Voice G. DB 6170/ED 357

HARRIS, Roy (1898-)
Soliloquy and Dance for Viola and Piano
  W. Primrose, viola / J. Harris, piano
  78 rpm—Victor Vic. 11-9212/3 set M 1061

HAYDN, Joseph (1732-1809)
Divertimenti for Baryton, Viola, and Cello (Barytontrios)
No. 95, Minuetto
  W. Primrose, viola / D. Stimer, piano
  (Arrangement Primrose and Piatigorsky)
  78 rpm—Victor Vic. 12-0698
No. 113, Adagio
  W. Primrose, viola / D. Stimer, piano
  (Arrangement Primrose and Piatigorsky)
  78 rpm—Victor Vic. 12-0698

HINDEMITH, Paul (1895-1963)
Der Schwanendreher, for Viola and Orchestra
  Columbia Chamber Orchestra / Pritchard / W. Primrose, viola
  Columbia ML 4905 / Philips ABL 3045/A 01132, 2
Sonata for Viola and Piano No. 1 in F Major, Opus 11, No. A (1922)
  W. Primrose, viola / J. M. Sanroma, piano
  78 rpm—Victor Vic. 11-0013/4 set M 547 (o.n. 15367/8)

KREISLER, Fritz (1875-1962)
Allegretto, in the Style of Boccherini, for Violin and Piano
Arrangement for viola and piano
  W. Primrose, viola / J. Kahn, piano
  45 rpm—Camden Cam. CAE 144
  78 rpm—Victor Vic. 10-1098
Liebesfreud, for Violin and Piano
Arrangement for viola and piano
  W. Primrose, viola
  78 rpm—Columbia C. DB 1585
Liebeslied, for Violin and Piano
Arrangement for viola and piano
  W. Primrose, viola
  45 rpm—Can. CAE 251
  78 rpm—Victor Vic. 12-0287

Praeludium and Allegro, in the style of Pugnani, for Violin and Piano
Arrangement for viola and piano
  W. Primrose, viola / F. Rupp, piano
  78 rpm—Victor Vic. 11-9614 set M 1131
Tempo di Minuetto, in the style of Pugnani, for Violin and Piano
Arrangement for viola and piano
  W. Primrose, viola
  78 rpm—Decca D. F. 1597

MASSENET, Jules (1842-1912)
Elégie for Voice and Piano with Cello Obbligato (E. Gallet)
Arrangement for contralto, viola, and piano
  M. Anderson, contralto / W. Primrose, viola / F. Rupp, piano
  78 rpm—Victor Vic. 10-1122 set M. 986

MENDELSSOHN, Felix (1809-47)
String Quartet No. 1 in E-flat Major, Opus 12, 2d movement, Canzonetta
Arrangement for violin and piano (Burmester), "Capriccietto"
  W. Primrose, violin
  78 rpm—Columbia C. 4633

MOZART, Wolfgang Amadeus (1756-91)
Duo for Violin and Viola No. 2 in B-flat Major, K. 424
  J. Heifetz, violin / W. Primrose, viola
  RCA Victor Vict. LVT 1014/LCT 1150
  J. Heifetz, violin / W. Primrose, viola
  78 rpm—Victor Vic. 18195/7S set M 831
Symphonie Concertante for Violin, Viola, and Orchestra in E-flat Major, K. 364
  Perpignan Festival Orchestra / Casals / I. Stern, violin / W. Primrose, viola
  Columbia 4 ML 4564 / Col. 33 WCX 1089 / C FCX 224 / Fontana Fon. 699012 CL/CFL 1013
  RCA Victor Orchestra / Solomon / J. Heifetz, violin / W. Primrose, viola
  RCA Victor Vic. LM 9802-E/LSC 2734
  New Friends of Music / Stiedry / A. Spalding, violin / W. Primrose, viola
  78 rpm—His Master's Voice G. ED 257/60 / Victor Vic. 18238/41 Set M. 838

NEVIN, Ethelbert (1862o-1901)
The Rosary (Rogers), for Voice
Arrangement for viola and orchestra
   Victor Symphony Orchestra / O'Connell / W. Primrose, viola
   78 rpm—Victor Vic. 18222

PAGANINI, Niccoló (1782-1840)
Caprices for Violin Solo, Opus 1
No. 5 in A Minor
Arrangement for viola solo
   W. Primrose, viola
   78 rpm—Columbia C. DX 665/DWX 1593 / American Columbia
   AmC. 7323 M

No. 13 in B-flat Major, "Devil's Laugh"
Arrangement for viola solo
   W. Primrose, viola
   78 rpm—Columbia C. DX 665/DWX 1593 / American Columbia
   AmC. 7323 M

No. 17 in E-flat Major
Arrangement for viola and piano (Andantino capriccioso)
   W. Primrose, alto with piano
   78 rpm—Columbia C. DB 1585

No. 24 in A minor, "Tema con variazioni"
Arrangement for viola and piano (Primrose)
   W. Primrose, alto / J. Kahn, piano
   78 rpm—Victor Vic. 15733

Concerto for Violin and Orchestra No. 2 in B Minor, Opus 7
Rondo à la clochette, "La campanella"
Arrangement for viola and piano (Primrose)
   W. Primrose, viola / H. Isaacs, piano
   78 rpm—Columbia C. LX 607/LWX 191/LOX 341/GQX 11025

RACHMANINOFF, Sergei (1873-1943)
In the Silent Night, Opus 4, No. 3, for Voice (Foeth)
Arrangement for contralto, viola, and piano
   M. Anderson, contralto / W. Primrose, viola / F. Rupp, piano
   78 rpm—Victor Vic. 10-1122 set M 986

RAMEAU, Jean-Philippe (1683-1764)
Les Fêtes d'hébé (1739). Tambourin en rondeau
Arrangement for viola and piano
   W. Primrose, viola / J. Kahn, piano (arr. Kreisler)

45 rpm—Camden Cam. CAE 244
78 rpm—Victor Vic. 10-1098

SAINT-SAËNS, Camille (1835-1921)
Le Carnaval des animaux. Le Cygne, for Cello and Piano
Arrangement for viola and piano
  W. Primrose, viola / D. Stimer, piano
  45 rpm—Camden Cam CAE 251
  78 rpm—Victor Vic. 10-1476
    Reverse Side: Myronoff: Caprice, for Viola and Piano

SCHUBERT, Franz (1797-1828)
Ave Maria for Voice, Opus 52, No. 6.
Arrangement for viola and organ, viola and piano (Wilhelmj), viola and harp
  W. Primrose, viola / V. de Tar, organ
  American Columbia, AmC. AL 33
  W. Primrose, viola / J. Kahn, piano
  78 rpm—Victor Vic. 15733
  W. Primrose, viola and harp
  78 rpm—Columbia C. DX 720 / American Columbia 7378 M
Litanei, for Voice (1818) D. 343
Arrangements for viola and organ, viola and piano (Ferraguzzi)
  W. Primrose, viola / V. de Tar, organ
  American Columbia AmC. AL 33
  78 rpm—Victor Vic. 11-9117 / Reedition 1946: Vic. 17623 in M 736
  / Vic. 17794 in M 757

TCHAIKOVSKY, Peter Ilyich (1840-93)
None but the Lonely Heart (Nur wer die Sehnsucht kennt) (Goethe), for Voice, Opus 6, No. 6
Arrangement for viola and piano
  W. Primrose, viola
  78 rpm—Columbia C. 7323 M/C. DX 665

VALE, F.
Ao pé da fogueira
Arrangement for viola and piano
  W. Primrose, viola / D. Stimer, piano
  45 rpm—Victor 49-0918
  78 rpm—Victor Vic. 12-1109

VAUGHAN WILLIAMS, Ralph (1872-1958)

Flos` campi, for Viola, Chorus and Chamber Orchestra (1925)
Philharmonic Orchestra / BBC Chorus / Boult / W. Primrose, viola
78 rpm—His Master's Voice G. DB 6353/5

WALTON, William Turner (1902-)

Concerto for Viola and Orchestra in A Minor (1929)
Royal Philharmon. Orchestra / Sargent / W. Primrose, viola
Philips ABL 3045 / A 00132 L / A 01132, 2 / Columbia ML 4905
Philharmonic Orchestra / Walton / W. Primrose, viola
78 rpm—His Master's Voice G. DB 6309/11

ZIMBALIST, Efrem (1889-)

Sarasateana, for Viola and Piano, from the Spanish Dances of Sarasate
W. Primrose, viola / D. Stimer, piano
78 rpm—Victor Vic. 10-1441/2 set MO 1242

232

Index

Page numbers in bold type refer to photographs.

233

236

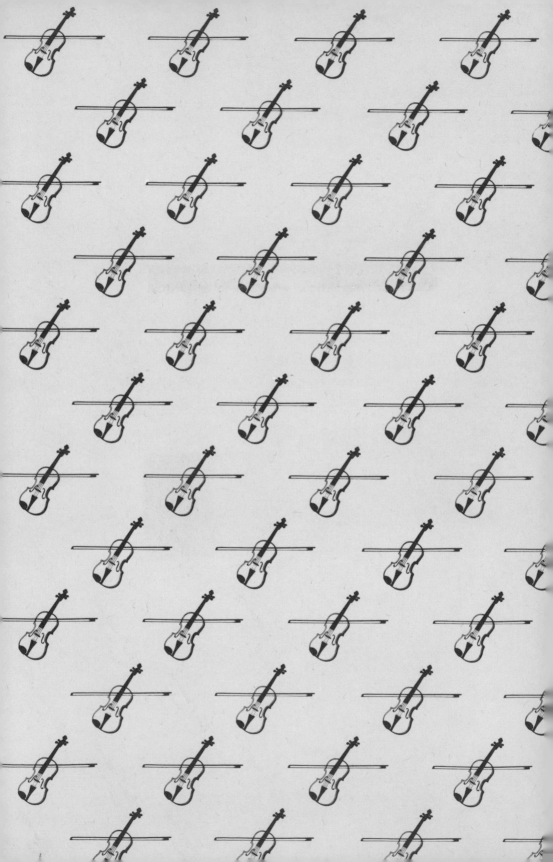